'A gift for pinnin[g]
all that comes his [way,]
the reader to share in his own
marvelling encounters.'
The Guardian

'Horatio Clare has the voice
of a great storyteller'
MICHAEL MORPURGO

'What Horatio Clare demonstrates,
beyond even his undoubted gifts as a
writer, is his basic humanity.'
PHILIP HOARE

'Light fills his writing'
The Economist

Published by *Little Toller Books* in 2025
FORD, PINEAPPLE LANE, DORSET

Typeset in Garamond by Little Toller Books

Printed in Cornwall by TJ Books

All papers used by Little Toller Books are natural, recyclable products made from wood grown in sustainable, well-managed forests

A catalogue record for this book is available from the British Library

ISBN 978-1-915068-45-3

We Came by Sea

Stories of a greater Britain

Horatio Clare

LITTLE TOLLER

Contents

For Esther, with love

Author's note

This book began in the winter of 2022 with a feeling of deep disquiet. People in small boats were crossing the English Channel day and night, whenever the sea was calm. They landed on beaches or were brought ashore by rescue vessels. There seemed to be just one story: 'migrants' were coming 'here', and this was taken to be a threatening, frightening thing. The country watched as this story was told with the same pictures and the same commentary, week after week. But when did a story ever have only one side?

It seemed strange that this one should be told only this way. It made each part seem uncertain. What is the 'here' that people are coming to? What kind of Britain do they seek and what do they find? Who were these people? How were they treated? What was being done for them and what were they doing for Britain?

What was and is actually happening in Dover and all over the country has a depth and humanity to it which is missing from the story of 'Channel migrants'. I followed its thread from Dover to Calais in the spring, and to Calais again in the autumn, and then to Falmouth and Portland the following summer, to Calais again in 2023 and then in 2024 to the north-west of England, and in 2025 back to Dover. And so this is only a small sliver of a journey through what seems to be a daunting and defining crisis.

There is no answer in this account to all the questions raised by migrations and refugees but there are truths here which contradict the way that these events have been framed. It matters that the frightened and frightening way of seeing these people and this issue should be challenged, because the individual heroism, the deep generosity, the humanity and the idealism that light this journey are signs of something much greater. It often feels as though we are living in a time of fear. If fear is not to subsume us, we must hear the voices defying it.

H. C.
Hebden Bridge, 2025

The people of vessels of every nation, whether in peace or war, are to be equally objects of this institution; and the efforts made to be in all cases the same as for British subjects and British vessels.

WILLIAM HILLARY, 1824,
on founding the Royal National Lifeboat Institution

With courage, nothing is impossible.
RNLI motto

The Voices

The security guard looks as though he is crying as the rain runs down his glasses but his voice is steady and warm. We are behind Lord Warden House, a shabby ghost of old England, white as a whale in the darkness, haunting Dover's Western Docks. Once a grand hotel, a favourite of Charles Dickens, George Eliot and Napoleon III, its shell now hosts the offices of freight firms. Visitors come for its parking spaces and the tents on the quay behind it. This is Tug Haven, where the people from the small boats are escorted off their rescue vessels. On the ramp up to the processing tents is where the photographers catch them. Thousands of people from across the sea, anonymous figures with their dark hair and orange life jackets, some wrapped in blankets, some carrying children, some children themselves, begin their new lives here. This facility will be attacked with petrol bombs, and the screening will be moved to Western Jet Foil nearby, but for now this is Britain's threshold.

Once they have been processed in the tents, people from the small boats are driven to a second fenced and guarded area where they await further processing, or just wait, until they are directed to a coach and driven up the hill and over the chalk cliffs to an England of motorways, outskirts, reception centres and hotels.

Between the processing tents and the holding area, the security guard is keeping an eye on a potential weirdo in a cagoule, wet jeans and soaking shoes, shivering at him. I am here in Dover because what is happening on the French coast and in the Channel, and in this town and behind these fences has become an obsession – for the press, for the politicians, for the people of Britain and for me. I have come here to try to understand it.

The Channel looked surly and thuggish at noon, the sea a spiteful yellow-grey under fog. Through the short dusk and into nightfall the wind has been bitter and inconstant from the south-west, spitting squalls of mist and rain. Surely, I think, nobody in a dinghy has tried to cross the Channel today. I hunch in my jacket, feeling awkward with the guard's eyes on me.

'Good evening!'

He looks uncertain. 'Can I help you?' he says. He is quite an elderly man.

'I'm writing about Dover,' I say. 'What do you think about the people in the small boats?'

And that is all it takes. As rain runs down his specs, the security guard speaks softly. He talks as though he has been waiting to tell someone this: 'I'm from Dover,' he says. 'Lived here 30 years. Retired. I came down here to see if these people are being treated properly. And they are. Really well. We can be proud – we're looking after them. We got an alert this morning – they cooked 200 sausages and then we had to eat most of them because it was a false alarm.

'There was a 26-year-old girl with a three-month-old baby on a night like this, January 4th. That really upset me. These people need help. And look at these fences! Look at the size of them. They're not going away – the world's on the move and politicians are not telling people the truth. I shouldn't be talking to you really.'

After a short while we say goodbye and I move away, bend

over my notebook in the gloom and write down what he said, and then I stand in the rain, amazed. I have only been here half a day and already the story that I thought I knew, the one everyone knows, has collapsed.

On the slipway earlier I met a jet-ski team from Border Force who told me they were trained and willing to do pushbacks out at sea. I was surprised, because according to the news and the narrative of this crisis, Border Force are preparing to go on strike rather than have their members risk prosecution for sinking dinghies. Ramming an overloaded inflatable crammed with people, which is what a 'pushback' means, could amount to attempted murder, so the union which represents Border Force is angrily opposed to it. But the jet-ski men I spoke to on the slipway are excited at the prospect. Some of them could not wait to get ramming.

'We've practised it!' one said. 'We know it works!'

'But what about the union?' I asked.

'We're not members of that union.'

'How do you feel about doing pushbacks?'

'I was in the Falklands,' said a senior member of the team. 'The mission then was "Get them off there!" If the mission now is "Push them back", this team won't have a problem with it.'

To this frank, stocky man with his Welsh accent and straight back, Argentinian soldiers had become people in small boats. They are *them*.

When I told them I was a writer they said they were not bothered about speaking to me, albeit anonymously. 'No one has been down here to ask us what we think,' said the Welshman with a shrug. We talked about their jet skis, and I mentioned volunteering on lifeboats when I was young.

'You should sign up!' the team leader said. 'You can find the application on the Home Office website. There's lots of jobs!'

They also said they sometimes turned their transponders off when they were out at sea. With the Automated Identification

System disabled, they could not be tracked.

'We switch it off when we're doing something covert,' said the youngest and most excitable. He refused to elaborate on that. Perhaps it was a fantasy. On the French shore, a young man dreams himself on the other side, safe in Britain. On the English side, a young man dreams he is some sort of commando, repelling Britain's foes mid-Channel. How many dreams soar over the Channel tonight, over this black and sloshing sea?

In London, politicians dream of resolving the crisis and news editors dream of milking it. Behind mansion gates, the owners of private outsourcing firms dream of ever bigger hotel-accommodation contracts and higher transport and custody profits (their dreams are real). Across the sea, smugglers dream of euros, sacks and bags and cases full of euros (their dreams are real, too). And across Europe, Africa and the Middle East, across the Earth, countless closed eyes have imaginary Englands flickering behind them tonight, Englands like Edwardian Lord Wardens in Edwardian sun, with sea views and tall windows. And here in Dover, the security guard stands in the rain beside the ghost of a once-upon-a-time hotel.

About this security guard: unless he is the only local person who thinks this way, what he has just told me is the whole story turning upside down. Retired Dovorians coming down here, taking outsourced jobs, donning the luminous uniform of Stand-Back and Do-What-You're-Told in order to make sure the people in the boats are *treated properly*?

Who knew he would say that? Where on earth is this side of the story? Where is this truth in all the millions of predictable and repeated words spouted about 'migrants in small boats'?

The politicians are not telling people the truth, he said. If his is not a lone voice, if this is not a marginal, uncommon feeling, then it is not just the politicians who are misrepresenting what is happening here. The media are not telling people the truth, either. Where have you read *Dover proudly welcomes refugees*? And if the media are not reporting what is actually happening, then the pundits do not know what they are talking about, and the interviewers are not asking the right people the right questions, or if they are, they are just reporting the same old story in the same old way.

It is not clear who is leading whom. Are the politicians simply reacting to the story the media is telling? If so, why are the media telling it this way? Because we look for crisis, for drama, for outrage, and manufacture it where we do not find it? Is it journalism's fault? If we are telling a skewed, unbalanced story, then the 'debate', so-called – the talk in the press, online, on social media and in our homes, pubs and workplaces – is awry. If this quiet, greying man is representative of how Dover really feels, what about the rest of Britain? Suppose this desire to help and protect and to take pride in helping is not limited to Dover. *We can be proud,* he said. But we are not proud.

Of course I am cautious. It might just be one man who thinks this way. And I am angry, too, because my hunch is that he is not alone, and if he is not then Britain is being taken for a fool.

We can be proud. We're looking after them.

Bloody hell.

I wish I could thank that security guard now, on behalf of millions of us who wish to be proud of Great Britain and Northern Ireland. I did ask his name.

'I wish I could tell you,' he said.

A dazzling winter daybreak blushes the white cliffs pink. Ferries sail across the sun's glare. They are not beautiful ships but they still carry something of the spirit of adventure, of foreign travel and the Continent, this lovely day. Flocks of herring gulls scream and spin over the harbour.

'We call it the bird ballet,' says a sharp-eyed lady, setting off for a freezing swim with her friend, both in wetsuits, hats and gloves. Dover looks almost magnificent this morning. As hotchpotch as its pebbles, as enduring as its castle, and run-down behind its seafront, it could be an emblem of Britain. During the Second World War this was the capital of 'hellfire corner'. The whole hinterland of east Kent was bombed, strafed and shelled. Monuments along Marine Parade recall the Dover Patrol, small armed boats, often attacked from the air, which rescued sailors and airmen from the sea. There are monuments and plaques to the Merchant Navy, to the soldiers and seafarers and the people of Dover who found themselves in the firing line and fought back. Something of that assertion and that defiance lingers in the fortifications, in the cliffs and in the ramshackle grandeur of the waking town. The gulls could almost be yodelling *Rule Britannia*, drunk on daybreak. You long to set sail from Dover on a day like this. You long to set out on a lifeboat, in fact.

I have worked with the Royal National Lifeboat Institution in the years since I crewed its boats. The charity is wonderfully open, helpful and enthusiastic, normally. It is still helpful and responsive, but recently its tone has changed.

'We appreciate the support and what you are doing but no, we can't take you out on a boat and we can't comment directly. Our CEO has put out a statement. You can find it on our site,' says a spokeswoman over the phone.

Not long ago the politician Nigel Farage came down to Dover Beach to be filmed accusing the RNLI of 'acting like a taxi service for migrants'. This was met with the outrage he hoped for – outrage from people alarmed by accounts in the press of 'fleets' of 'migrants', outrage from racist trolls, and outrage from those who were so appalled by Farage that they responded by sending donations to the RNLI. The charity recorded its best-ever fundraising year.

Coming in from the sea on a lifeboat with people saved from the Channel and their rescuers would be a vivid way to tell this story, I suggest to the spokeswoman.

'Impossible,' she says, and explains that the RNLI is trying to stay out of the politics of the situation, which means saying nothing to the press and telling their volunteers not to talk. 'And in any case,' the spokeswoman adds, 'they are recovering so many people they do not have space for a writer on the deck. Sometimes we're so busy we don't even count them.' I make a note not to use her name in anything I write, lest I expose her to abuse. It seems incredible in a free and democratic country that to report the name of someone working for a voluntary emergency service is to put that person and the service at risk.

Down at the Dover Lifeboat Station, the walls are covered with plaques recording RNLI rescues dating back to 1837. There is a telling blank where the recent records of achievement should be. Crew come and go, walking swiftly, heads down. During my time as a RNLI volunteer, we strode or sprinted down to our station with such pride and excitement. Volunteer crews have always felt this way. Even when the weather is abominable and you are scared of the conditions you are about to face, you are beyond proud to be with the boat, honoured to be trusted by the others on the crew. Crews are under no obligation to launch; the RNLI is independent of the state and the Coastguard. When coastguards identify a vessel or a person in danger they contact the RNLI, give the position of the casualty, as far as they know it, with whatever facts they have, and request a rescue.

Come the gales, come the monstrous, murderous seas. For the sake of strangers in peril, volunteers leave safety and go into it. Few people who are not professional sailors will experience the fury of the sea. But that terrifying power is what the boats are designed for and the crews trained.

On the RNLI's memorial in Poole to men and women who have died attempting rescues there are over 600 names inscribed. The last lifeboat lost at sea was the *Solomon Browne*, which launched under the command of Trevelyan Richards from Penlee Lifeboat Station, Cornwall, on December 19 1981. A small bulk carrier with a crew of five had suffered engine failure in a hurricane – Force 12 on the Beaufort Scale, the winds up to 90 knots, a 100 miles an hour, and waves up to 60 feet high: 18 metres. I have been on ships in severe gales and frightening swells but I struggle to picture waves the size of six-storey buildings. The little ship was being driven towards the cliffs. There was no doubt what was going to happen to her. It defies belief that people would put to sea in such conditions, but the crew of the *Solomon Browne* set out. Trevelyan Richards refused to take one person, the son of another of his crew, judging the risk too severe to take two members of the same family. The *Solomon Browne* managed to get four casualties off the doomed ship in a second pass, the waves so big that during its first attempt they dumped the entire lifeboat on top of the stricken vessel. Both were destroyed and all souls lost. The pilot of a rescue helicopter, helpless to assist, saw what happened. He wrote:

> The greatest act of courage that I have ever seen, and am ever likely to see, was the courage and dedication shown by the Penlee [crew] when it manoeuvred back alongside the casualty in over sixty-foot breakers and rescued four people shortly after the Penlee had been bashed on top of the casualty's hatch covers. They were truly the bravest eight men I've ever seen.

These are the people and this is the organisation that Farage and his followers bate and troll. And this is why being on the crew of the Dover lifeboat, until now, was to be counted among the best of your community, someone prepared to risk injury and death to stand for those in mortal danger. Dover Lifeboat Station has just taken on thirteen new volunteers and they are still recruiting. But I watch the Dover crews now, walking to their shifts with their heads down, their eyes averted.

I approach a coxswain, a man who looks phlegmatically prepared for a passerby's comments. 'It must be a strange time to be you,' I say, and tell him what I am doing.

'I wish I could talk openly,' he murmurs. 'It's incredibly rewarding to help people, of course. In Dover we're always the front line. Wars, refugees, migrants – that's what it is here. And I've seen the faces of people ashore who wish you weren't doing what you're doing.'

Being unable to speak freely frustrates him. The last time I wrote about a place when I could name nobody, for their own sake, was in Turkmenistan, an insane dictatorship floating on hydrocarbons and despotism. And this is Dover.

For days I walk back and forth, stopping people, asking questions, seeking glimpses into the thoughts of strangers. Everyone seems happy to speak and no one wants to be named.

'What do you think about the small boats from France?' I ask.

'We never see them,' smiles a retired teacher walking her dog. We talk a little and she says she loves living here. 'It's all kept very quiet,' she says.

It is, too. You have to take circuitous routes even to glimpse the lifeboats and Border Force boats bringing people into Tug Haven. And everything after that takes place out of sight, unless you stand where I met the security guard last night, where you can just about glimpse people being escorted to unmarked buses. There is one other viewpoint near there, the place the photographers go to, but I am working up to that.

'You can't have *everyone* coming in,' says a local man collecting pebbles that his wife likes to paint. 'But we'd do the same, wouldn't we?'

He tells me his daughter-in-law works for an organisation that helps asylum seekers.

'When they tell her they want to take their own lives, that takes a toll on her,' he says.

'It's not the best situation,' says a Dovorian in his 20s, walking a Labrador puppy. 'But we'd do the same.'

His companion, also local, agrees. 'We would do the same. I feel sorry for them,' she adds. 'My mum's got a job with Border Force.'

I find a Border Force agent hauling on his dry suit in a harbour car park. This man's team recover the smugglers' dinghies which would otherwise be abandoned at sea after rescues.

'You can't identify me,' he says, urgently, when I tell him I am a journalist.

'I promise I won't.'

'We're the RAC,' he grins. 'We do the long slow tow.'

When he looks at the people in the small boats he sees irrationality, he tells me, more than anything else.

'It feels mad,' he mutters, his expression suddenly pained. 'They put themselves in danger. If you put your wife and children on one of those dinghies at sea, you'd be charged.'

'Would you do pushbacks?' I ask.

'No! Can you imagine? Doing that to a flimsy boat at sea? It turns over, people drown.'

'But I met a team of Border Force with jet skis yesterday who seemed quite keen to do it.'

'We're the local office,' he sighs. 'They're national. We should be pushing passports. But instead. . .'

And with a shrug he sets off to search, rescue and tow.

★

Everything I can see and everything these people are telling me fits with what the first security guard said. Dover is not, as sections of the media have it, 'overwhelmed by migrants' or 'up in arms' or feeling frightened or threatened at the small boat crossings. On the contrary, Dover is sympathetic, understanding and doing everything it can to help the people in the boats.

I go back to Tug Haven, back to the fences and the uniforms, where a guard in luminous high-vis, blocking the entrance to the processing tents, turns out to be another retired local man. He says that a group of people have just been brought ashore.

'They're safe now!' he smiles. He looks really happy. 'There are very young children with them. They're being looked after. I come down from Ramsgate for a twelve-hour shift – and you're doing your bit, aren't you? You want to see they're alright. Because they must be desperate, mustn't they?'

I suggest that 'Doing your bit,' is the language of the Second World War, of heroic national effort.

'Yes it is!' he says, as proud as a grandfather.

'May I ask who you work for?'

'I can't tell you that,' he says.

It does not take much to find out. His employers are Mitie Care and Custody. Running processing and holding centres has boosted Mitie's 'Care and Custody' revenue to £60 million, a £10 million increase the company ascribes to 'small boat arrivals on the South Coast'.

Mitie Group's overall revenue is up 103 per cent to £1.9 billion. By the end of March 2024 this will have ballooned to £4.5 billion, with the 'Care and Custody' division raking in a rapid fortune of £217 million, made from detention, removals, processing and transport at some of Britain's most notorious sites, including the infamous Manston Processing Centre.

Migration is not normally framed as a blessing to business, but it is. I watch jolly employees of HATS (a patient transport company), Interforce (a security company) and Loyalty Connections (a

Kentish coach company), alongside police, Home Office and privately contracted medical staff all going about their work, in and out of Tug Haven. The general impression is an air of bustle these docks cannot have known since the fishing industry died. Shouts of laughter and good-humoured greetings are constant; they were last night, too, when it was cold and raining. The sense of common purpose, of meaningful endeavour, of 'doing your bit' is palpable. Even standing around in your high-vis, guarding in the cold and wet on minimum wage seems to make your spirits lighter and your smile freer when you feel you are helping the destitute and detained.

Everything you think you know about Dover and the 'migrant crisis' is wrong, I think, watching. But the fear it provokes is real.

The CEO of a refugee charity pleads with me when I call: 'Just call me a spokesperson?' A lady walking her dog also requests anonymity, though she waives the dog's right: his name is Max. Even the armed forces are scared to speak.

I contact the Royal Navy. In an effort to be seen to be doing something, to appease the right-wing press and its constituencies, presumably, the government has announced that the Navy will take overall control of events in the Channel. The Navy, the word comes back, will absolutely not speak about the situation or take me to sea. It is unclear what they are supposed to do about the dinghies, anyway. They could mount rescues with their tenders, but warships are primarily designed to blast boats and people into the deep, not pull them out of it. The Navy has no formal relationship with the RNLI, which will continue to work with the coastguard.

Another golden morning turns into a sparkling winter day, the sun high, the air ringing with light. From the top of Shakespeare Cliff, to the south-west of the town, you can see the whole story laid out below you on the sea. Here are the ferries, the castle and cliffs. The sky is Battle-of-Britain-blue. It even buzzes with a Merlin engine as someone flies over in the two-seater White Cliffs Spitfire Experience. There is Dover lifeboat, launched on exercise. They are working up the new crew today, coordinating with a rescue helicopter which hovers low above the sea. We did that once, taking turns to manoeuvre our boat through the aircraft's down-draft of whipped spray to be winched up and down. It must be an unforgettable day for the fresh volunteers.

Over to the east is the low line of the French coast, from where the small boats set out, aiming for the UK border, mid-Channel. Although France retrieved over a thousand people from its waters last year, the French authorities have found it is difficult and dangerous to interdict the dinghies. They are not deterred by warships or patrol boats. Once the dinghies are at sea, the French vessels cannot stop them or turn them around without the risk of sinking them. Last week one ignored a French warship, refusing to stop until Dover lifeboat pointed its searchlight at a Union Jack on the superstructure of a Border Force vessel, showing the frontier had been crossed. Another dinghy got into difficulty off Berck-sur-Mer. A Sudanese man in his twenties died.

The impotence of the French authorities, once the boats are launched from the beaches, leads to accusations in the British press that France is merely escorting the small boats out of its waters. It is hard to see what else France can do. If the dinghies get into trouble, the French can rescue them. Otherwise they stand off, keeping a safe distance until the boats reach British territory.

As they putter across the sea, the dinghies are tracked by Dover Coastguard, liaising with French authorities at Cap Gris-Nez. Helicopters, drones and spotter planes use thermal imaging to count people aboard.

The British government has given a billion-pound contract to a Portuguese company to run maritime surveillance drones in the Channel. Their cameras are able to film the faces of the people, some picked on the beach and some drawn at random from each dinghy's passengers, some of whom have ended up steering the boats. These people can now be prosecuted for trafficking, though they are surely not the traffickers. Sometimes the trafficker will offer a reduced fee to those who will steer the boats. The Coastguard designates each dinghy a 'radar target', and gives its position to search and rescue vessels which bring the people in them to Dover Western Docks.

The astounding thing is how successful this semi-joint operation by France and Britain has proved to be. In perilously unfit boats, helmed by men with no experience, tens of thousands of people in substandard or no life jackets, many of whom cannot swim, have survived a notorious stretch of sea and one of the busiest shipping lanes in the world to be recovered and landed safely in England. There have been disasters, but they speak more harshly of the British government, which has been cutting back funding to the Maritime and Coastguard Agency, and thereby reducing the numbers of skilled coastguards, than they do of the the people trying to coordinate and effect the rescues.

The volume of boats crossing the Channel in the days running up to the tragedy of November 24, 2021, overwhelmed the understaffed Dover control room. On November 20 just three operatives tried to deal with 110 reports of small boats. On November 24, staff seem to have downgraded emergency calls, apparently out of desperation, in a kind of fingers-crossed hope that the number of rescue vessels and the number of dinghies at sea would somehow match up. There were just two people on operational duty that night. One of them was a trainee. The RNLI were not tasked to attend the incident. The French and British coast guards told people in the stricken dinghy who were begging for their lives that they were in the other country's waters. At least 31 people drowned, all of whom could and should have been saved. Robert Jenrick, Immigration Minister, made a comment on the disaster which surprised MPs across Parliament: 'We will not be able to secure the passage of everyone who chooses to get in an unsafe dinghy,' he said. The youngest victim was Hasti Rzgar Hussein. She was seven years old.

And yet, given the sheer numbers of people who have been rescued from this sea, there has been no operation like it since the evacuation of the British Expeditionary Force from Dunkerque in 1940.

You could see it, as the press and politicians do, and as the British people are being taught to see it, as a crisis, a disaster, an intractable knot of problems with no clear solutions. Or you could see it as one of the greatest search and rescue success stories of all time.

Imagine *those* headlines. *Dover saves another sixty from the sea. Record-breaking Day of Rescues. Combined Operation Saves 45,000 this year.*

Would we feel differently about this country, about the people in the small boats, and about ourselves, if we were reading this every day? And the fact is, it *is* true. This is what we are doing. This is us.

2

The Newsman

I still cannot understand why no one has been telling the story the way it is unfolding. But the next morning I return to Tug Haven, to the press photographers' vantage point, the place where all the pictures of huddled people wrapped in blankets coming off the rescue boats are taken, and meet a man who makes some sense of it. He tells me he is a self-employed photographer and reporter, a one-man news agency. The newsman has been a regular here a long time, he tells me, feeding the papers. His car is his office – laptop, phones, cameras and cables strew the seats. He has a jangled, almost manic air about him.

'*The Mail, Times, Telegraph,* yeah! The *Sun* don't want it so much – they're trying to clean up their image, aren't they?'

It turns out that slews of daily reports and pictures from Dover in the British press have come straight from this man. I look up his pictures and the lines he takes on the stories he sends to the papers. The long-lens camera he wields (and the identical pictures sent in by other photographers, when there is a surge or a tragedy) are the eyes through which Britain is seeing this whole situation this winter. To a significant extent, I realise, it is these pictures and this framing, adjusted by the news desks at his customer newspapers, which gave me the feeling that something was wrong with the way the story is being told down here.

'How do you get the stories?' I ask.

'Well, I've got a VHF radio listening to channel zero and channel 16 [these are the frequencies used by the rescue services], but even if they raid my house, they won't find it because it's at my mate's place. Rigged it up so it sends the audio direct to my phone. I live halfway between here and London so when I hear something kicking off, I can be down here by the time the boats come in.'

We chat away. Occasionally he breaks off to hail the crews of Border Force vessels setting out for sea.

'You're early, aren'tcha? Miss breakfast at the Premier Inn?' he shouts. 'Nice day for it!' he grins, firing away at them with the camera.

Eavesdropping constantly on the emergency frequencies, the newsman listens as ships are diverted around rescues. He follows rescue missions when thick fog or high waves complicate operations. He records the numbers of people recovered, and how many of them are children, and he knows when anyone is in particular danger because he hears the reports from the lifeboats and Border Force vessels as they radio Dover to put medical staff on stand-by. Then he comes down here to Tug Haven and photographs the arrivals as they are disembarked.

'It's been crazy!' he says, happily. 'Most of the time it's just me here. Did you see the pizza story the other day? That was me.'

His pictures of discarded pizza boxes led to headlines including *£6,000 Dominos bill to feed migrants at Dover*. He has a seller's eye for the media's appetites and he is proud of his success.

'My headline this morning was *Migrants Play Lifeboat Roulette*,' he says, and explains that he listened to Dover and Dungeness lifeboats, tasked by the Coastguard but blinded by thick fog, becoming confused about which was covering which small boat. 'They got in a right muddle, both heading for the same one.'

I give no sign that *Migrants Play Lifeboat Roulette* strikes me as a misleading way, at best, of framing an incident in which desperate people were saved by expert rescuers in deadly conditions of fog, waves and darkness.

'How does it make you feel, doing this?' I ask.

'Oh, I'm definitely desensitised!' he says, cheerfully. 'If there's no murders on in London I come down,' he grins.

When I say I have been surprised by the care and kindness everyone I have spoken to feels towards the people on the dinghies, he switches. Suddenly he is agreeing with me:

'It's the compassion. That's what I notice. How careful they are with them. The way they help the women and children, they're really gentle.'

It seems that there is nothing in his thinking or his motives beyond attention and cash. The money, he has found, is in demonising 'migrants' and slanting his stories to generate fear and hostility towards them – and so he does, which may be how the news and picture editors of the newspapers he supplies feel, too, when they run his stories and pay him off.

And so it seems that this tale is enclosed in a clasp of two malign sides. One is the drama of the 'invasion' narrative stoked by certain politicians and some sections of the media. At Dover railway station a huge billboard dominates the platforms, advertising GB News as 'the people's channel'. Daily, GB News deals, it seems to me, in what the far right calls 'migrant hunting', along with comment and punditry apparently designed to fan the flames of fear and hostility around refugees and migrants, all decked out – nauseatingly for real journalists – in the trappings of journalism and wrapped – shamefully for genuine fans of Great and greatly diverse Britain – in the Union Jack. Commentators at GB News appear to champion the asylum policies of Denmark ('Denmark and Poland just showed Britain exactly what needs to be done to tackle the migrant problem', writes Adam Brooks on 30 March 2025):

the Danish government has implemented various policies to discourage immigration, including demolishing public housing in designated 'ghettos' and requiring the children of immigrants to attend 25 hours a week of Danish language childcare, away from their parents. Since 2016, people caught attempting to cross the Danish border to claim asylum have anything of value taken by border guards: watches, jewellery and even wedding rings are seized by the state and set against the cost of the asylum system. These policies have worked: setting aside Ukrainian refugees, numbers granted asylum in Denmark have fallen from 10,000 in 2015 to 860 in 2024.

To those owners and operators of the media that frequently focuses on anti-migrant narratives, the people in the small boats are now 'aliens' from different cultures – by definition illegal – who deserve nothing but hostility and deportation. As GB News may, arguably, exist to prove, stacked in anonymous heaps under lurid headlines, desperate people with complex stories can be turned into living stairways, ziggurats of thousands of bodies and interchangeable faces, up which wealth-friendly politicians and populists can be marched to power.

The second side of this tale, empowered by the first, is the abuse and mistreatment of individual human beings: the men, women, children and families who are the 'migrants', 'asylum seekers' and 'refugees'. Examples could fill a book, or thousands of pages of a judicial enquiry: institutionalised abuse at Brook House Immigration Removal Centre, near Gatwick; horrifying conditions at the Manston processing centre (families were billeted on wet cardboard and made to eat on muddy floors, and suffered racist abuse and assaults by guards); sickening conditions at Napier Barracks, Folkstone; sexual abuse and inhumane treatment at Yarl's Wood Immigration Removal Centre – and these are only the stories which reach the press.

Beyond them are thousands of incidents and hundreds of complaints of bullying, mistreatment and harassment of people who are waiting in hotels and accommodation run by outsourcing firms on behalf of the Home Office. The agonies of mental ill-health, self-harm and suicidal ideation are endemic among the population in detention centres and asylum housing, in the estimation of Refugee Action, among other groups. It gets worse. Over 1,300 refugee children have been wrongly assessed to be adults by the Home Office, according to the Refugee Council, and forced to share rooms with adults, leading to abuse.

There is no room for good news in this dark binary, or much hope of more balanced news. There is no space for compassion or decency. But the normal everyday good that is also the truth of this story runs all through it, unsung, unspoken, so quiet it is all but silent. I am not the only one asking questions in Dover; a team led by the Independent Chief Inspector of Borders and Immigration, David Neal, is here, too, looking inside tents I can only see from the outside. His report on Dover's official reception of the people from the Channel is easily summarised: 'Overwhelmed ... inexcusably awful ... not good enough ... system failure ...', but his team of inspectors also watch and talk to the same people who talk to me, and they and Neal are touched by what they find:

> Staff on the ground are doing their very best, but they
> are tired. The workforce can do no more. They have
> responded with enormous fortitude and exceptional personal
> commitment, which is humbling, and they are quite rightly
> proud of how they have stepped up.

The problem is that no one reports that side of the story and the staff themselves are forbidden to speak of it.

3

Speech and silence

At least one person in Dover is unafraid to go on the record about the small boat crossings. Kay Marsh, 'Dover born and bred', has a look which is assessing and indomitable. She gazes straight at you with a wary frankness. In a town full of people doing their best to help those arriving in need, among hundreds of Dovorians who have been cowed into silence and anonymity, Kay will speak out all day.

'When that boat sank last year, I gave interviews to journalists around the clock for a week,' she says. 'I never stopped. Barely slept! What do you want to know?'

Kay is a well-known figure in the town, a human rights activist and a volunteer with the Samphire charity, who is unbowed by abuse from the far right. They are a tiny and impotent sect, in her experience, 'But with a very, very loud voice.'

She volunteers at Napier Barracks, a holding centre in Folkestone run by an outsourcing company called Clearsprings. Clearsprings will take £500 million in British government contracts for accommodating asylum seekers in 2022; the owner, Graham King, an Essex businessman, will personally bank £25 million in pre-tax profits. In 2024 *The Sunday Times* will put his personal worth at £750 million. A joint investigation by *Prospect* magazine and Liberty Investigates calculates that Clearsprings, with Home Office contracts for asylum accommodation worth £23.4 billion, took over one in every twenty pounds of the Home Office's *entire budget* for 2022/3. Perhaps it is not surprising that Napier is a hellish place. You do not make that sort of money without knowing how to economise. David Neal's inspectors judged Napier impoverished, run-down, unsuitable for long-term accommodation and filthy: 'People at high risk of self-harm were located in a decrepit "isolation block" which we considered unfit for habitation,' they found. *Prospect* notes that mortality rates among people in the asylum system are significantly higher in Clearspring facilities.

Kay was appalled but unsurprised by the squalor, the mental-health crises among residents and the Covid outbreak she first found there.

'It's a bit better now,' she says, 'but it was the staff who really surprised me. I'd prejudged everyone. Just like you can't judge the boat people, you can't judge the staff. Jobs like G4S, contracted from the Home Office, they're low-level jobs that people can *get* – and the staff are genuinely nice people. They're making a difference to people's lives, they really are. The people in charge don't give these organisations a good name. The Home Secretary is not representative of the people who work here.'

We talk about the profile of people like her, who help. The Border Force crews are mostly men, the security guards are mostly men, men outnumber women on the lifeboat crews. 'But once you get behind the front line, is it true that the people who run the charities, who go into places like Napier to give help and support, are mostly women?' I ask.

'It's true!' Kay exclaims. 'If you see a man volunteering at our support projects he's normally there with his wife.'

This lodges in the back of my mind – *mostly young men in need of help, mostly women helping them* – but it is not until I reach Calais, a couple of weeks later, that it becomes a starkly striking fact. When Kay goes to work, I go back to Tug Haven to see the people from the small boats being brought ashore.

They are so present in the media as a strange and hostile force – and so absent as individuals – that it is almost like seeing celebrities when I finally glimpse them through the wire. First the clothes they have arrived in are loaded onto their coach in plastic bags. Then the people appear, track-suited, wrapped in red blankets, shuffling in white flip-flops. One woman carries a child. A man carries a toddler. There are several young men, boys, all moving in the same exhausted drift.

However hard you look, it is especially difficult to discern individuality in the boys. With their Covid masks, similar short haircuts and similar tones of brown skin, they just look like 'migrants', as we have been taught to think of them. It seems extraordinary that a couple of hours ago these dazed figures were an almost insanely daring group of travellers, squatting together on a tube in a dark and heaving sea.

They come out of the tents in ones and twos, moving very slowly. The fear and adrenaline of the crossing has drained to a dragging exhaustion. The relief at being well treated when they arrived must have come like a wave over them. After the threat and rush on the French shore, being given something to eat and a health check must have made them feel cared for and drowsy. They board the coach as if they are going to sleep in its warm seats for a week.

There are security guards at the door of the bus, and one, a woman, chats happily with the driver. I cannot tell what they are saying but the body language and the laughter make it an easy, funny conversation. I watch as the guard welcomes each traveller to the coach. She steps back and gestures gently, with a small, after-you sweep of her hand, ushering the people aboard. It is moving to watch that gesture, and the way the guard and the driver treat the passengers with welcome and concern. The passengers slump in their seats. Some look out of the windows blankly, some shut their eyes.

When no more people come from the tent, the coach is driven slowly across the car park to another fenced-off area. The gates are drawn shut behind it. The passengers disembark, beginning an odyssey through the British asylum system which may take years of their lives. You can watch them all you like, but you will not hear them. There is so much silence here, and that silence tells the story of what is happening in Dover, silence and hushed tones.

To lower anyone's voice in Dover, just ask, 'What do you think about the boats from France?' The threat of being sacked, or reluctance to be identified with a particular view, and fear of abuse and threats from the right seem to govern every tongue. Free speech is choking in Dover. If you wish to know what is actually happening here, and allow them anonymity, then the rescuers, guards, emergency services, enforcement agents, officials, seafarers and locals – the people who are the voices, hands and faces of this astonishing chapter of Britain's history, the interpreters and enactors of national policy – have much to reveal about 'the migrant crisis'.

No one I speak with uses that phrase. All-engrossing to those involved, the Channel crossings are all but invisible to everyone else. Following events here through the newspapers and websites supplied with photographs by people like the newsman, I had assumed that all the security, expense and effort along this coast was a response to some kind of threat, some sort of security breach by 'illegal migrants'. The truth, as far as the people involved are concerned, is precisely the opposite. Dover is busy, even booming, and Dover is trying to help.

★

Walk along Marine Parade to the dreary end where it peters out at the crossing point, where the promenade meets the truck-stormed highway into the docks, and you'll see on a low wall at knee level two black marble plaques with gilded letters. One, in English and Chinese, says, 'In memory of 58 young people from China who died near here on 18th June 2000 – All human life is precious.' The other reads, 'In memory of the many victims who have lost their lives seeking sanctuary in the UK.' It is dated October 2018 and ends with a quote: 'Every migrant has a name, a face, and a story – Pope Francis.'

The placing of the memorials is strange, almost embarrassed. The low wall was there already, holding back a flowerbed. It is as though the people who put the plaques up feared antagonising anyone who might object or vandalise them. They huddle at the very edge and end of the town, almost hidden. No one has vandalised them.

Towns, individuals, groups and even nations can be prejudged. The tone and language with which the British government and media frame events in the Channel and on this coast led me to expect outrage, nationalism and xenophobia around Dover, which voted strongly for UKIP and Brexit, and in 2024 will transfer some of those votes to Reform, which comes in second after Labour. Instead, everywhere, I find people from every sort of background, holding every shade of private view, whose strongest feelings for the people in the small boats is compassion, whose instinctive reaction is to help, and whose efforts are extraordinarily dedicated and effective. What amazes me most about the hushed voices of Dover is how proud they make me feel of Britain.

4

Calais before spring

Even on a wet February night, the centre of Calais suggests a richer, happier town than Dover. There are chic shops, bars, boutiques and ateliers, restaurants, a smart hotel, wide squares, free buses. The edges of Calais tell another story, of chronic unemployment, poverty and crime at levels which surpass Dover, one of the most deprived towns in Kent, but the features of a once-prosperous town are still here. On the beach, shuttered huts are drawn up in ranks on the sand like roosting gulls. The lighthouse waves white arms at the Channel. Here and there are figures with plastic bags, lowered heads and quick eyes, young men from far away, heading out of the centre towards the fringes, to wherever they are sleeping tonight.

The owner of my guesthouse is an owlish man who loves rugby and tradition. He wants us all to assemble for supper and hold conversations between the tables as we make our way through the courses, a vision of hospitality which must stretch back to the France of his grandparents.

I ask him what he thinks of the rough sleepers. Aware of the attention from three couples at the other tables, he ponders and answers seriously.

'They don't affect us or the business,' he says. 'We don't have any problems with them. Here in the town we have many CRS [Compagnies Républicaines de Sécurité – riot police] and cameras. On the edges, it is different.'

He tells stories of stolen food and break-ins, but they seem vague and uncertain. 'Hundreds of trees have been cut down so they can't make their camps in them,' he says. 'It's sad to see the trees go.'

Of the situation, he says, with a shake of his head, 'C'est compliqué.' The word carries more freight in French than 'complicated' does in English. 'Compliqué' means vexed, twisting, unhappily intertwined.

I will come to know Calais in the coming days and years. The felled trees are the least of the transformations this town has undergone. People began coming here in the 1990s, refugees from wars and state violence in Kosovo, Iran, Ethiopia, Eritrea, and from the Kurdish areas of Iraq and Turkey. They aimed to cross the Channel in trucks on ferries. The opening of the Channel Tunnel in 1994 offered another route. By 2001, EuroTunnel reported it was repelling 200 people every night.

Razor wire and security guards bloomed around the Fréthun freight terminal where the trucks drive onto tunnel trains. People from Africa, the Middle East and the Indian subcontinent made mass attempts to storm the railway lines, the ferries and the truck roads. They were fought off by riot police and security guards, and in one instance by a ferry crew who turned power hoses on them.

Double and treble lines of five-metre fences topped with razor wire were erected along the railway tracks and around the harbour. More fences went up along the roads leading to the port, more along the feeder roads and roundabouts leading to those roads, and more beneath the bridges to stop people sleeping under them or climbing them to avoid other fences. It has taken thirty years and untold hundreds of millions of pounds and euros to raise the fences of Calais.

A walk to the town centre from the ferry terminal in the new expanded port is a tour of miles and miles of steel mesh where flocks of cameras oversee galaxies of razor wire. The views are abandoned parking areas, derelict walkways and the shuttered buildings of older port infrastructure that proved too small and too easy to penetrate. Thousands of tonnes of rocks have been transported from quarries south of the town and deposited around the outskirts of Calais, blocking access to places where charities used to distribute food. Reefs of tumbled stone fill in sheltering arcades around abandoned buildings to prevent people sleeping out of the rain.

The fortifications look complete for now, dystopian in their scale and vacancy, defending bare spaces. You walk along a road with impregnable fences on either side but beyond them there are mirrored lines of more fences – at the roadside, at the foot of an embankment, then at the top of the same embankment, line after line, one behind another behind another in metallic mirages, a claustrophobe's fever dream.

All of this made it much harder to stow away on a ferry or a train, though around 9,000 people a year continue to reach Britain in trucks, a number that has varied but not much changed over the last five years. Then, in 2018 the first small boats crossed the Channel from France. In 2019, over 1,800 people made the journey that way; in 2020 more than 8,000; in 2021 over 28,000; in 2022 over 45,000; in 2023 over 29,000; in 2024 over 36,800.

All the fences, all the rocks, all the cameras, all the guards and all the miles of razors dangling on coils of wire have successfully diverted over 150,000 women and children to board small boats across the sea.

The charity's warehouse is in the western suburbs of Blériot Plage, named after Louis Blériot, an inventor, engineer and industrialist who gained worldwide fame as the first man to fly a plane across the Channel. Naturally, he had a grand dinner at the Lord Warden before he took off. Blériot Plage answers Dover's memorial to Captain Matthew Webb, who in 1895 became the first man to swim the Channel, the second to cross it in the water. Earlier the same year, Paul Boyton floated, scooped and swam his way across from Boulogne to Dover using a prototype wetsuit-drysuit and a paddle, his invention disqualifying him from the swimming title. Today's descendants of Webb, Boyton and Blériot have attempted the same feat in inner tubes, kayaks and pedalos. One man tried using a rubber ring and flippers. People on both side of the Channel, the French and British publics, celebrated these crossings made for sport, adventure and invention as brave heroism. Crossings undertaken now, for life, for family, for hope, are seen as desperate and desperately unwanted at best; at worst, as threatening and criminal.

Blériot Plage is a long, busy road on a winter morning; the murals of gulls and shuttered guest houses have the same feeling as parts of Dover – a holiday world where holidaymakers no longer come. The warehouse is an L-shaped cavern piled with pallets of donations. Hillocks of tents, jackets, shoes, blankets, toiletries and sleeping bags are stacked high and in such profusion that it would take a regiment weeks to sort the rubbish from the reusable. The charity does not have a regiment. It has a semicircle of a dozen or so volunteers, young people and the retired, mostly women, mostly British, who make tea and prepare to receive their instructions. Both the leaders this morning are young women. One gives the briefing.

'There are no migrant camps in Calais,' she says. 'There are only illegal settlements. We're going to be distributing jackets and sleeping bags. We're going to put out the charging boards and the generator so that the refugees can charge their phones. We'll set up the football goals and the tables with Connect Four. It is really important that we control the distribution. You will have to watch out for people cutting into the line, or coming back twice to get more than their allocation. You can just be friendly but firm if that happens. You need to take your IDs because the police will sometimes make arrests. If that happens, keep a note of everything they say to you and everything that happens. If you are assaulted, take pictures of any wounds or bruises. Stick together, keep an eye on each other, make sure you are always wearing your Care4Calais high-vis. So, I need volunteers for each one of these roles.'

She starts to take the names. My guide this morning will be Gessica Lastrucci. She does not look delighted to be guiding a writer. She drinks coffee and smokes a cigarette. She is pale and not tall and her features have a set about them, something vivid and directed. By the irritable hunch of her shoulders, she needs to be elsewhere. In her jacket, leggings and robust trainers she could be a young professional, perhaps a lawyer, about to set out on a run. I explain what I am doing. She shrugs.

'So many journalists come, and they ask so many questions, and nothing changes. These people are not stupid, they read the websites, they know what people say about them. Maybe they don't trust you. Maybe some do. We will see.'

We set off in a battered van. She drives like an Italian, fast and tightly, working the old van's gears. Little by little her story comes out.

'I grew up near Florence. My family are farmers. I didn't get any qualifications. Then I saw the refugees and I have to help. I went away for two years, worked on cruise ships to get the money to live here because the charity cannot pay me. I live in a caravan, sometimes I stay in a squat in the town centre.'

'And your name – it's Italian?'

'Ha! My mother liked the name Jessica but we don't have it in Italian with a J, so she made it with G. I think I'm the only one!'

We hurtle around another mini-roundabout. Industrial estates and retail parks spin by. It is strange to think that this ugly and anonymous world is a destination for which people risk everything, and that these hems and offcuts of Calais are the last step before that paradise of the imagination, Britain.

I explain to Gess that I have come here to ask the question repeated everywhere since significant numbers of refugees and migrants began attempting to reach the United Kingdom in 2015: Why do these people want to come to Britain?

The media have reported various answers but, like the refugees and migrants and charity workers, like the far right and the politicians who whistle to them, I do not trust the narrative to give a full and nuanced picture of the truth. For an introduction to the refugees, I contacted the Care4Calais charity, which has been distributing aid here for six years. Gess is the charity's scout and ambassador, its eyes and ears, a one-woman front line.

Gess responds with a briefing on the situation, delivered in rapid, emphatic and Italian-accented English.

'This morning we're hunting white people!' she laughs. 'If it comes out of my mouth it's not racist. We're looking for Afghans and compared to the Sudanese they look white – so.'

Her clothes smell of woodsmoke, rain and burned plastic. We park up near a hospital and set off across a bleak stretch of wasteland.

'The Afghans are hiding. They used to be the biggest group here but now the Sudanese are the biggest so they have taken the best places. The best places are near the truck parks or the motorway. The groups fight each other – Afghans and Sudanese hate each other. I know there are Afghans here somewhere, maybe hundreds, but where? I need to find them so that we can reach them, otherwise they have no access to clothes, food, tents, nothing. If I cannot find them, we cannot make a plan for them.'

We set out across the wasteland. Grass in fat yellowish clumps, scattered litter and rough paths, sawn-off tree stumps, a cold wind and two horizons of motorways comprise this 'best place'.

Gess walks fast. She gives the impression of never having enough time. She limps, having broken her right foot in Ventimiglia on the Italian border with France, where she was helping people before she came to Calais.

We cross rough ground; some small stands of trees remain. Here the people hide. The refuse and the remains thicken underfoot as we approach. Now we are moving through shoes, pill-packets, ragged remains of tents and tent bags, rusting cans, toothpaste tubes, sleeping-bag stuffing, bottles, rotted trainers, cartons and toothbrushes.

'This was the Jungle,' says Gess. 'It was cleared. It's been cleared many times. This is left over from evictions.'

Both the rubbish and the people are left over from evictions. Now we are picking our way through human faeces. There is a wincing chemical reek of smoke. Now everywhere there is rotting food and discarded clothing and there are people smiling and saying 'Hello!'

A stubborn line runs through my head: *This is what the apocalypse is like*. It is melodramatic but probably about right. When we lose everything, this is how we live. The dereliction upsets you at a core-deep level. Civilisation separates roads, tents, wasteland, toxic smoke, people, faeces and rubbish. Here they are all compacted, strewn around and thrown together. The endurance in people's faces and the listless hunch of their backs and heads is somehow horrifying and outraging. This horrible place cannot be acceptable, you think, absurdly. How is this allowed to be? What has happened to us, to France and Britain and Europe, that all we want to do for these people is make this place *worse?*

What do you do in the midst of such squalor? You welcome your guests, of course. A man invites us to sit down in the small stand of scrub where he hides his tent. The police make daily sweeps, seizing anything they can carry away. His friend's tent was taken yesterday, the man says.

The man does not want to talk to me. Instead he offers tea. To make tea in a slum of bushes and rubbish on the outskirts of Calais on a wet February morning, you first need a plastic milk carton. You cut it in half, then carefully set fire to the sawn-off edge. Dioxin-rich smoke reeks upwards. The plastic becomes molten and drips, and you catch these molten drips on the driest piece of wood you have, and this is now your firelighter. You set fire to that melted plastic that smokes evilly and you thrust it into your little wigwam of drier twigs. The fire takes, producing a little pall of wet and toxic smoke and a small bloom of flame. And now you put a can of water on.

The men who emerge from the bushes are young and friendly. They move slowly, looking tired and demoralised. The hopelessness of the scene is palpable and ought to be pervasive, amidst squalor where you could never be quite dry, never quite warm, never quite comfortable. But now Gess goes into battle.

'Hey!' she cries, 'You!' She throws her arms around a young man, and hugs him. In a moment he is laughing. 'OK?' Gess asks. 'What's wrong with your shoes? Oh my god, where's his tent?'

'Police,' the young man says.

'When?'

He and his friend were not here when the police came yesterday, the young man explains. The police time their raids to coincide with food distributions. One of his friends saved his tent from them, picking it up and walking away, but he could not carry the other tent, too, so the police took it.

'Mushkila!' cries Gess. 'I come back tonight. I bring shoes. And he needs a tent.'

'Mushkila', Arabic for 'problem', is the word I hear most often in the following days. Gess never says it without a grin. She never gives the impression that problems cannot be quickly overcome.

Gess stays as long as she can, speaking 'refugee English', a rapid kind of dialect everyone understands. The young man who offered us tea pretends not to understand my questions.

'Why should he trust journalists?' Gess demands, as we hurry to the next fire. Each time we find another group, she shouts greetings at them gleefully. She hugs many, with proper full-on hugs. She punches them and grapples. She questions them and harangues them. She finds out how they are, where others are, what has been happening to them and what they need with astonishing speed, rigour and acuity. She is so busy fooling about and shouting that the men – they are all men and boys – hardly realise what she is doing. By the way she behaves, and by the way they instinctively raise their spirits, their senses of humour and their morale to meet her, you would think they were all university classmates.

I would not feel easy going into some of these places by myself in daylight. Gess is making promises to return tonight. I ask if she is ever scared. She is affronted.

'Scared? Scared of what? These are good people. They always try to protect me. If a white girl goes by herself to them at night, that shows them they are not scary, they are not different. We are all the same. It humanises them.'

In the afternoon Gess drives us to 'Old Lidl', an expanse of desolation, bare earth and puddles. The French Red Cross are giving out tea and coffee. The Infobus charity is handing out leaflets about rights, aid and the danger of sea crossings, and providing charging for mobiles.

The CRS riot police stand around the fringes, looking blankly on, as about two hundred refugees and migrants, overwhelmingly Sudanese, mill about Old Lidl in an excited crowd. The CRS are quite a sight. They wear armoured shoulder pads and arm-guards, gauntlets and armoured leggings which protect their knees, shins and feet. Their flak-jacketed torsos and belts bulge with equipment – gas, cuffs, pistol, baton, radio. A long cavalcade of fifteen vans and cars, sirens and lights on, disgorges forty officers.

A freedom of information request to the Home Office reveals that although the British state does not directly fund their salaries, it does provide money for their equipment. Strictly speaking, the Home Office admits it 'holds information' regarding Britain's contribution to equipping the CRS, but refuses to disclose it on grounds of security and diplomacy: a classic non-denial.

The police cavalcade circles the town, pulling up at the four main inhabited wastelands to make daily raids on the tents, sleeping bags and possessions of the rough sleepers. The presence of the file of officers adds an edge of threat and challenge to the atmosphere. The crowd seems excited, gleeful and defiant.

Gess runs in and whacks a friend, who is soon chasing her. Grappling, headlocks and delighted shouts follow. Nearby a large flock of black-headed gulls scream – not the happy seaside sound, but a frantic feeding screech which is the soundtrack of this bare place and the large squalid settlement in the trees. There is a film crew from *The Guardian* newspaper, and me with my notebook, and something about the day, the energy of the gathering, the cold blue sky and the clouds hurrying overhead seems to energise us all. The loitering police, in armour designed to terrify, look on.

'Education!' says Hamza, a bright and amused young man from Sudan, when I ask him why he wants to go to Britain. 'When I have children, I want them to go to school there.'

I push him. Surely it is crazy to risk his life for children he does not have.

'In UK it is better,' he says, determinedly. His friend agrees. Their friend agrees. A semicircle of young men forms.

'It's incredibly expensive!' I say. 'The food is terrible and it rains all the time. Why not stay in France?'

Britain is not racist, they tell me. It is a fair country, a good country. They know people there who tell them it is better.

It is better is the mantra. Everyone clings to it and asserts it.

'But it's going to be hard,' I say, 'and cold and difficult, isn't it?'

'Yes,' Hamza says. 'I know it is going to be hard, but it is better there.'

'How are you going to get there?'

'Truck, truck, truck!' he grins. No one here can afford the smugglers' boats. Everyone is trying to hide in a truck.

'They try,' Gess says. 'They don't make it, they try again, they get tired, maybe wait, they get depressed, many months, then they try again. But yes, it's worse when they get to Britain. Here they have each other. They are together, they can see friends, travel to Paris or Brussels on the train. In Britain they will be alone, poor, no information, no help, many problems. But if I tell them, they don't believe. So I just –,'

She shrugs and looks, for the first time, helpless. 'I just keep their dreams alive.'

In years of writing about elite police units, soldiers, seafarers and rescuers, I have never seen a display of leadership and motivation to touch what Gess does that day, and every day. The British Home office has recently sent £55 million of UK taxpayers' money to fund the policing, fencing and maintenance of this hostile environment. And yet this one vibrant Italian woman, and the aid network behind her, add more to the refugees' morale than the police are able to subtract. You could argue that Gess, her peers and the charities are costing the UK millions. But take her, them and the aid away – the food bags, shoes, water, tents, firewood, coats and clothing, charging points for mobiles, toothbrushes, sleeping bags and SIM cards the charities provide – and you still have 3,000 young men sleeping rough around Calais and Dunkerque, only more miserable, colder, hungrier and more desperate. It is hard to see that going well. The French state makes the same calculation, allowing one charity, Secours Catholique, to provide one hot meal a day.

Later that day, we visit another site and start hunting through reed beds for Afghans, Gess limping. As each day goes on her foot hurts more. She does not slow. We learn the CRS are making a sweep. We rush to a bare fringe of mud and rough grass known as Rue de Judée. Thirty young men, their tents and sleeping bags piled in their arms, stand sullenly on a corner. Forty riot police, formidably equipped and armoured, trudge through the scrub. A small white truck follows them. Every now and then, the police stop, scoop up tents and sleeping bags and throw them into the back of the truck. There are two unattended tents under an unfelled tree and we can all see what is about to happen. Gess rushes towards them. She is going to try to save what she can but the police arrive a moment later. A woman police officer tells her to move away and leave the area.

'I don't speak French!' Gess cries, not moving. CRS officers close in, herding us back to the road. You can feel the force and the threat of violence emanating from their armoured shoulders. It comes off them like a kind of heat. I walk with them. One looks at me with loathing. If I would just slow down a little more he could give me the push he is longing to unleash. I keep pace with another who seems less tense.

'How do you feel about doing this job?' I ask.

'I can't talk to you,' he says, and his grimace speaks for him.

They throw the tents into the little truck. Three French charity workers struggle out across the rough ground towards the remains of the encampment. They are college-student age, a woman and two men, fighting to push wheelbarrows loaded with firewood over rocks and tussocks. They and Gess are upset by the police sweep and the taking of the tents, and the police know it. The police, too, seem humiliated, resentful, almost ashamed. There is a bitter and unresolved feeling in the air. As they climb back into their vans, one of the CRS shouts, 'On est chez nous!' 'It's our home!'

Enraged, the leader of the firewood gang, a young woman from Lille, shouts back: 'It's our home too, asshole!'

By the end of the first day I am exhausted. As I retire to my B&B, Gess is limping through the dark back to the first man we visited, to eat with him and his tentless friend, to raise morale, to keep their trust in her.

Clare Moseley, the founder of Care4Calais, chooses an odd place to meet. She is not known in this anonymous black-panelled café-bar on the Place d'Armes, Calais' main square, which is good, because certain places and residents in this town do not welcome her. Clare does not give a damn. Tall, wrapped in a winter coat and scarf, she asks for a Jack Daniels and coke, her voice surprisingly quiet and light, with an up-turned lilt at the end of her sentences in which you can hear Merseyside.

'I was an accountant,' she says, 'I was 45 and I didn't know *anything* about this situation. I was living in Liverpool with my husband. And then one Saturday morning I read about refugees drowning in the Mediterranean. I couldn't find a charity to donate to, only a small group going to Calais to take supplies, so I went. And here I am!'

She laughs, but in Calais she found refugees asking desperately for food and a man carrying his baby who begged Clare to take her – to take the baby with her to Britain. Clare never returned to her former life. Within a few weeks she had started the charity, rented a warehouse, recruited and organised 60 volunteers and was providing aid to many of the 6,000 people who were sleeping rough. The numbers swelled to 10,000 and fell, over the years, to the few thousand who are here now.

In that time Care4Calais became a significant force in Calais, in Dunkerque, in Britain and in the asylum and migration debates between Britain and France. It seems that no national or international development in the saga of the migrants and refugees is now reported without a quote from the charity giving its views, which remain dauntlessly committed to the rights and wellbeing of refugees and migrants.

Care4Calais' lawyers have stopped deportation flights, prevented people being transferred to barges, pursued French and British authorities over what they did or did not do when people drowned at sea, taken the government to court over the conditions in which asylum seekers are held in barracks, and fought countless individual actions. In France, they won the legal right to distribute food to the rough sleepers. Clare, who barely speaks any French (she tells me, with another laugh), has made a decisive impact on the lives of hundreds of thousands of people and the conduct of policy of two major European powers.

As you would expect, Care4Calais and Clare have been scorned, abused and denigrated by politicians, attacked by the right-wing media and pilloried by innumerable trolls. But when the government in Britain and its outsourcing companies are stuck, they quietly turn to Care4Calais. Indeed, Clare says the charity's work is in even greater demand in Britain than it is in France.

'The Home Office calls us and says they've got hotels full of desperate people who've got nothing, who don't speak English, the outsourcing companies can't help them – can *we* help them?' she says. 'They become convinced their claim is going to be rejected and they just lose hope.'

So Clare sends someone into the places she calls 'asylum blackspots', where dozens or hundreds of asylum seekers are living in or being thrown out of hotels and accommodation, where there is barely any charity coverage, where one volunteer for Care4Calais may be able to help, may be able to go in, organise translation, rally scant resources, reassure, obtain small items, explain what is happening, stop people falling into despair.

Clare's vision for what we should be doing has a simplicity about it which sounds almost naive until you remember that you are talking to the person who has seen perhaps more than anyone else the realities of Calais and the UK asylum system, and who turned her distress at reading one article into an international rescue effort and a charity which is one of the most serious players in the whole asylum debate.

'So what should we do?' I ask her.

'Safe and legal routes. If we give people safe and legal routes to claim asylum in the UK, they won't have to cross the Channel and the smugglers will have no business model.'

'But what are they going to do when they get to Britain?' I ask.

'If we had put all the money we're spending on the hostile environment here and in the UK, all the billions of pounds we are spending on the asylum backlog, on the hotels, on the holding centres, on Rwanda, on all the security, if we had put *all that money* into investing in infrastructure and jobs in the deprived areas of the country, *imagine* how different that could be. And people who got asylum could do some of those jobs. Imagine if you invested all that money in the North East. '

'What should we do about the backlog?'

'Clear whole countries. Iran, Syria, Afghanistan – these countries have acceptance rates of 95 per cent and higher. So clear them. Check them, yes, but clear them. Hire more Home Office staff. I think the government could clear the backlog in no time, but I think their donors in the outsourcing companies don't want them to. They're making too much money.'

'But if that's true, that would be PPE mark two,' I say, referencing the obscene fortunes made during the Covid pandemic by firms with links to the Conservative Party.

'Yes, well I think that *is* what it is.'

Clare's advice to Britain on our best policies for asylum and migration might seem idealistic, but in a few weeks' time Russia will invade Ukraine, and Britain will provide safe and legal routes for Ukrainian refugees, clearing the whole country, effectively, in a scheme which will start in some disorder but will rapidly become a model of how a refugee scheme can work, admired around the world. Imagine: *British refugee policy admired around the world!* But that is exactly what happens.

The following morning I talk to young men in a food queue near New Lidl. Rain is falling, everyone has wet feet, and yet people are laughing and joking as they wait for coffee and bread.

'Britain abolished slavery,' a Cameroonian says, when asked why he wants to go there. A man from Guinea says Britain is fair, not racist, better than France.

Speaking with a charming young Guinean sociologist who is resolved to cross the Channel hiding in a truck, I find myself saying, idiotically, 'You're going to need to be so strong if you make it – the anxiety of waiting for a decision on your application.'

He laughs. 'We are all experts on managing anxiety,' he says.

In the afternoon, we go back to the Rue de Judée for another distribution. This time the police target the volunteers. A bright and authoritative officer backed up by two armed juniors tells the charity volunteers they do not have the right to hand out aid here today.

Clare calls her lawyer and the police call their superiors. She explains to me that the Calais authorities aim to hamper aid efforts by switching the permitted distribution points at short notice. The police take my press card to radio in its details. Nobody else seems to speak English and French, so I find myself translating between the police and the charity.

'What's it like to do your job here?' I ask one of the officers.

'It's not why we joined the police, but it's the mission,' he says, heavily. Like the rest of the CRS, he says, he is billeted nearby. He tells me he will be here, far from his wife and young children and their home in eastern France, for months.

One of the volunteers hisses that the police are racist, fascist thugs. It is true that police officers have behaved in terrible ways in Calais and Dunkerque. Individual officers have been found guilty of assaulting refugees and charity volunteers, and fabricating evidence against people who accused them of these acts. But these three men are not racist, fascist thugs. They are just cops, doing their jobs amiably, I point out.

'If you knew what violence they do, you wouldn't think like that,' the volunteer retorts.

The call comes back from the lawyer. The charity *does* have the right to distribute in Rue de Judée today. The police officer checks with his superiors and has Clare sign a piece of paper, a copy of which he then gives her.

I thank the officer for his help.

'No need to thank me,' he says, briskly. 'It's the law.'

The law now resoundingly on their side, the charity workers start giving out tea and biscuits; out come the games and the phone-charging boards. A queue forms for haircuts as one of the men takes over the clippers and scissors and starts trimming. At the same time, another CRS unit plods down the road behind the site to a stand of trees. They raid another settlement there.

The scene takes on the weirdest double aspect. I watch the rough sleepers encouraging and hugging each other, asking the charity for aid for their friends, translating and running errands for one another. The older and more confident help out the younger and those with the least English. And here, too, are the volunteers, young and old, giving their time and care: here is kindness, here is generosity, here is hope.

And over there are people in uniform who signed up to serve France, to protect society, the innocent and the vulnerable, and who find themselves consigned to taking away tents and sleeping bags from homeless people who have next to absolutely nothing. In their CRS outfits, festooned with intimidating kit, these men and a few women find themselves being paid and ordered to inflict further misery on some of the most helpless and vulnerable people in the country.

Of the two groups the police look strikingly morose, while the rough sleepers, whenever they gather for a distribution, generate an extraordinary positivity. They are living abominably marginal lives, yet the soundscape they generate when they come together for food and aid is laughter. There is vivid energy in the constant turbulent movement of people messing about and joking in the queues for handouts, in the scratch football games and cricket matches, and at the Connect Four tables.

In fact everyone here is vulnerable to this situation; everyone is harmed. It turns out that the suicide rate among the French police forces is 36 per cent higher than the general population. Should the people queueing for handouts ever reach the United Kingdom, research by the Refugee Council suggests that 61 per cent of them will experience mental illness as they wait in a limbo queue, years long, for decisions on their applications.

The situation is beyond absurd, and yet none of this is a failure or an accident. Everything here is planned, legislated and funded into being. Britain does not want these people (though the majority will be accepted for asylum, if ever they get the chance to claim it) and France does not want them here.

The two countries have decreed the daily attacks on the

camps by the police, the felling of sheltering trees, the dumping of rocks, the raising of fences, the constant pressure to prevent these people settling, to deny them comfort, ease or security. This degrading, humiliating upshot is modern Franco-British immigration policy in action. This policy might seem less bizarrely cruel if Britain did not have a labour shortage, a falling birth rate and an economy which would benefit from the efforts and industry of these courageous people.

The marvels of Calais in February are the determination and resilience of the refugees and the people who help them, and the poverty of the political imagination behind policies which keep them here. I found answers to my questions. People want to come to Britain because it is better than where they are, and better than where they have been. But why Britain should be so expensively resolved on crushing the energy and hopes of so many who wish to give everything they have to a country they believe to be so very special, I do not know. The brutal cruelties of our policy, which are everywhere here, seem to have become ends in themselves. Nothing we have done to these people has succeeded in its aims. Judging by all you see here and all you hear, none of this persecution, violence or abuse will stop them, or the boats.

5

Calais before winter

In November I return to Calais, to write about what is happening there and what has changed since February, when Russia's invasion of Ukraine drives an eventual 267,000 people to apply for British visas. The visas are granted. Government gives funds to councils, which pass the money on to hosts. Ukrainians are welcomed everywhere. Blue and gold Ukrainian flags appear across cities and villages as people open their doors to strangers from far away. The British people raise an uproar in the early days of the war when it appears that their country is failing to offer effective help to sufficient numbers of Ukrainians. The national conversation flames with indignation at the inefficiency and obduracy of the Ukraine visa system. In Parliament on March 14, a member of the Cabinet, Michael Gove, hurries to respond. He defends what has been done, and then adds, 'We also know that the unfailingly compassionate British public want to help further.'

He announces the Homes for Ukraine Scheme, and ends with this:

Our country has a long and proud history of supporting the most vulnerable during their darkest hour. We took in refugees fleeing Hitler's Germany, those fleeing repression in Idi Amin's Uganda, and those who fled the atrocities of the Balkan wars. More recently, we have offered support to those fleeing persecution in Syria, Afghanistan and Hong Kong. We are doing so again with Homes for Ukraine. We are a proud democracy. All of us in this House wish to see us defend and uphold our values, stand shoulder to shoulder with our allies, and offer a safe haven to people who have been forced to flee war and persecution. The British people have already opened their hearts in so many ways. I am hopeful that many will also be ready to open their homes and help those fleeing persecution to find peace, healing and the prospect of a brighter future. That is why I commend this statement to the House.

And the House of Commons cheers.

You cannot help but wonder how a speech like this would change the way Britain feels about itself and the people from the small boats, if it was made in their support. Many of the Syrians and Afghans it refers to came here in dinghies. Debates break out: Why do we treat Ukrainians differently from other nations? Is it because we watch what happens to their country in real time, as Russia invades? Is it because they are Europeans? Is it because they are not Muslim? Is it because Ukrainians are overwhelmingly not brown or black? Is it because we see it as a straightforward case of Ukraine as victim and Russia as aggressor, a whole-story simplicity we cannot attach to Syria, Afghanistan, Eritrea or Sudan?

Ukraine has been attacked by a war criminal, and we experience none of the confusion or uncertainty that most of us would feel if asked to explain the histories and conflicts driving people to flee Afghanistan and Syria, and Britain's role in those countries. Brits do not hesitate to open their doors to Ukrainians, a surge of national feeling that affects our attitudes to the rest of the world, too. A YouGov poll finds that 71 per cent of Britons support resettling Ukrainian refugees in Britain, 50 per cent feel the same way about Afghans, 48 per cent about Syrians, and 40 per cent support resettling Somali refugees here.

It turns out that we are surprisingly open to people coming to Britain to work or to relocate with their families. In 2022, YouGov finds clear majorities in favour of both – 39 per cent are in favour, while 30 per cent against people coming to work, and by 38 per cent to 24 per cent we feel favourably about people relocating with their families. But 55 per cent of those polled held a negative view of those crossing the Channel, rising to 85 per cent among Conservative voters.

Right here, in this discrepancy, is the result of years of political aggression and condemnation, years of demonisation of 'migrants', years of stories in the papers that people like the Newsman feed, years of photographs of huddled, anonymous figures in dinghies, years of denigration and hostility poured on them by some in the right-wing media. This is the truly 'hostile environment' – a hostile environment of the mind. The targets of the hostile environment were and are, ostensibly, migrants and 'illegal immigrants', but it has no deterrent effect on them, as their numbers show.

As the issue becomes more poisonous and obsessive in the following years, driven by hysterical headlines and popularity-seeking politicians, the public responds: up to 50 per cent of those polled tell YouGov in 2025 that immigration over the preceding decade has been 'much too high'. Yet the people who are crossing the Channel come to seek asylum, and in the main they are right to do so, given that the majority are found to be genuine refugees and are granted refuge: 66 per cent in the year to September 2024, according to the Home Office. They wish to work and those who have families wish to relocate here with them. But a great political and media effort seems to have ensured that they are not seen this way. And so the real targets of the hostile environment, the targets who have been struck and changed, are us.

Blériot Plage in winter is a dark doleful line of houses, their backs to the wind and sea. The brightest light is the supermarket, where a harried cashier charges a line of residents for small baskets of shopping and swears under her breath at the local drunk. From the window of my room, Calais is sleety outlines of hard-shuttered houses, battened against the night. The idea of being out there in a scrappy wet tent is enough to make you draw the curtains and think about something else.

At the Care4Calais warehouse in the morning, there are the same rickety vans, the little troop of volunteers, and there is Gess, attending the morning meeting. The briefing is given briskly and thoroughly by Lucy, a manager. She begins with the official script.

'There are no refugee camps in Calais, there are only unauthorised settlements and distribution points. We have tents and sleeping bags donated from festivals in the UK which we need to give out. We need to sort the ones that we can use from the ones we can't. We are expecting a big eviction at one of the biggest sites in Calais.'

Gess seems dazed. Sitting apart, holding a mug but not drinking, she stares into the distance while Lucy lays out the plan. Sorting in the warehouse in the morning will be followed by a distribution in the afternoon. Gess looks haunted, exhausted, barely there. When we set out to visit the rough sleepers, Gess driving the battered van, I ask her what has happened, what has changed?

It pours out of her in the nearest thing to a monotone her Italian cadences can render. The whole scale of her speech in February, which ran from shouts and yelps to cries, orders, demands, amazed commentary, laughter and fury, has gone, flattened.

'In the centre the police go twice a day now. They change days and times, sometimes morning, sometimes evening. We are running out of stuff – no one can keep up with giving everything to everybody. If the guys are there when police come, they can carry their stuff, but the guys never know when to expect them. If the police catch them trying the trucks, they beat them. If someone is hurt, the police refuse to call the ambulance. On the 30th of October a lot of people tried the boats. Five boats didn't make it – people were in the water. One person I know lost his brother. The coastguard said they saved everybody but I *know* he was in the boat and he never came back. We went to the hospitals in Boulogne, in Calais. We went to the coastguard and checked with the police – they launched here, from Sangatte. His mother has been crying for weeks. I had to ring and tell the family.'

We pull up in a side street near one of the illegal settlements. Gess stares out of the window of the old van as she speaks. I think she is seeing the faces and names of people she is talking about. I am scribbling notes. Gessica's face has lost none of its determination but her distress, her exhaustion and her absolute honesty are almost frightening. There is the sense that everything superfluous, anything remotely trivial or self-caring has been seared off her. I remember something she said the first time we met: I asked her what she did to relax – did she go out with friends? Which bars did they drink in? She looked at me with incomprehension.

'Go to bars? No? What for? Why I would want to do that?'
'To wind down – to take a break?'
Her expression was eloquent in its complete dismissal.
'Do you ever go home to Italy? See your family?'
'I have, but – it drives me crazy. People talk about things like their jobs, their houses, they complain about money. About

money! You have a *house*! You have money! Don't you know there are people who don't have anything – and you *complain*?'

It was suddenly easy to picture her among her family and their friends at the dining table, where so much of Italian life takes place, radiating incredulity.

Now she shakes her head. 'Calais is a nightmare. It's a trap,' she says. 'So many arrive here normal, but people lose their minds here.'

'Are you still in touch with people who have made it across?'

'Yes. When they reach there I get so many calls, the situation is terrible, they're treated badly, some of them even say they want to go back to Calais.'

'What about Rwanda?' I ask.

That summer there was an attempt to load people on a deportation flight to Rwanda. Care4Calais, alongside other charities, organised lawyers for the detainees. The flight was cancelled on the night it was due to take off. Rwanda is a nightmare too far, the Home Office calculates. Rwanda is the barbed-wire crown on the miseries already endured by these people. Rwanda will break them. Britain hopes to impose experiences so unpleasant on those who succeed in crossing the Channel that their stories will overcome the common belief in the country as the better place, deterring future asylum seekers.

And so Calais is a battle of dreams. Can the dream of the life you imagine be overcome by the hostility of the environment you find here, and by the nightmare of a deportation you could not bear?

'Rwanda just made people want to cross faster,' Gess says. 'They didn't care about the wind and the waves, they just wanted to go.'

She tells me the threat of Rwanda drove a wave of panic through the rough sleepers. 'There were two suicides, one Ethiopian, one Sudanese. One lay on the tracks, another hung himself in a container.'

She looks so hurt, so defeated and exhausted that I want her to go back to the caravan where she lives and sleep for a month. She never will. Her phone jars constantly with appeals for help and she refuses to switch it off. She is not being paid for her work by Care4Calais. Her job, the one she actually does, does not even exist. No one could be asked to go into the scratch camps and the rough sleeping areas, day and night. No one else would give out their phone number to the refugees. No one else will call the families of the disappeared. Some of the people who pass through Calais on the way to England may have more money than Gess does, but not the ones she is most dedicated to helping, the people who cannot pass through, the men and boys who get trapped between the wastelands, the trucks and the sea.

'Do people know what it's like in Britain?' I ask, as gently as I can.

'I tell them the truth but they don't believe it. Nothing can stop them. Even the truth doesn't stop them.'

I ask Gess to describe the situations of the different nationalities, the refugee map of Calais. Each settlement has an unofficial name, she says, and a rough ethnic make-up. Old Lidl and Auchan are mostly Sudanese. Others are Old Jungle (Afghans, Iraqis, Iranians), Hospital Jungle (Afghan), and Unicorn (a mix of Ethiopians, Iranians, Pakistanis, Egyptians and Moroccans). While most are scrappy tent clusters partly hidden in thickets, Town Centre comprises Syrians, Afghans, Yemenis, Iraqis and Iranians sleeping under bridges. It is raided frequently, but it offers access to the boats.

'Arab, Afghan, Syrian, Yemeni, Iran, Iraq, they have word of mouth, friend to friend,' Gess explains. 'They come, they go, they have a plan. You never see an Afghan face for more than a week or two weeks.'

'How does that work?'

'For example, the Sudanese refugees have no money so they help find people for the boats. They do all the dirty jobs, work to find people, get the money, give it to the smuggler. If anyone is caught it's the refugee. They go to prison, not the big boss.'

'On the beach there is another hierarchy,' Gess says. 'Those paying full fare, 2,000 euros plus, get a place on the boat. Poorer people pay less to go stand-by.

'If there's no space you wait, because you can only pay 800 to 1,000 euros, so you go to the beach many times and there is no space, so you wait.'

We get out and walk over to Old Lidl. The settlement has shrunk since I last saw it. Men and boys crouch around fires below a motorway horizon and above a ditch. Old Lidl is now a line of tents balanced on bits of wooden pallets, scattered around with torn fragments, bottles, old trainers, cartons and refuse.

Efforts are made to keep it in order – tins are stacked in a rusty heap, the path is clear, and the cooking fires have makeshift seating. Squatting around the fires, men and boys look up, see Gess and grin their greetings at her. They are overwhelmingly Sudanese. Along with the Eritreans camped at the site known as BMX, they are among the poorest groups. They do not have money for the boats but there are dozens of them, and so they occupy this ground because it offers access to the motorway, where lorries occasionally slow, and trucks stop, which can occasionally be broken into.

'I know one man who broke both his legs trying the trucks,' Gess says.

As the rain falls the men wait – for the next distribution, for the next police raid – and they hope. Waiting and hoping are Old Lidl's specialities. It's hard to know whether to cheer at the resilience of the human spirit or despair at its quixotic insistence. Either way, in the residents' imaginations, Britain in the winter is as bright as it was in the spring.

Gess is greeted with shouts of welcome, waves and grins. One man asks her for a phone. Another for a sleeping bag. 'Yes,' she says, 'OK, I will find out and I will come back and find you.'

I cannot ask questions because her standing and, therefore, the safety and effectiveness of what Gess does may be compromised if the people she is helping discover that she is talking to a journalist. The British press does not have a good reputation on the derelict fringes of Calais.

We return to the warehouse, where the volunteers are preparing for the afternoon's distribution at Rue de Judée. The volunteers here accrue stories of people's motivations. John Adams, who will be on tea and sugar duty at the distribution, says one man told him he was inspired by *Inspector Barnaby*. 'It's the title of *Midsomer Murders* in Germany,' Adams says. 'That's where he'd watched it and that's why he wanted to go.'

The distribution is executed with speed and verve, in defiance of the bleakness and the cold. The vans pull up, the volunteers pile out. They erect a table with Connect Four games, temporary football goals, a makeshift cricket pitch in the form of blue plastic stumps, a generator and charging board for phones, a haircutting point complete with chair, cape and clippers, a tea and coffee point, and they organise a queue for sleeping bags.

There is something queerly British about the games, the queues, and the way Afghan cricketers and Sudanese footballers ignore both the downpour and the row of police vans which arrive and disgorge riot-armoured officers. In the milling crowd of the rough sleepers and volunteers, I circulate, and now I can talk to them.

'People only need to have some little hope,' says an English graduate from Sudan, when I ask if he thinks he will make it across the Channel. The rain thickens, darkening the mud. I start shivering. He notices, laughs and says, encouragingly, 'A little hope is more than none!'

The weather is vicious, which brings a kind of grinning solidarity, as we all hunch slightly under the cold rain.

'But why England?' I ask him.

'Because the English understand us,' he says. 'They have understanding of our history and our situation. They know about Darfur and Blue Nile province.'

I fail to contradict him. Instead I ask, 'Have you heard of the economic crisis in Britain?'

'Of course! The rich nations are poorer and the poor ones are *really* poor,' he says.

And of course he knows about the Rwanda scheme, too. It has not deterred him. 'We do not know our destiny! Only God! If someone has some hope, he will do anything,' he says. 'My father said, "If you wake up, your body is OK, if you have some little bit of food, then you are OK. You can help others." I think this is what life is for. Here I help people with language, with translation.'

Now the police are trudging towards a scrap of woodland to sweep it for unattended tents. As they do every time, a small knot of men stands watching them mutely, holding jumbles of wet camping gear in their arms. I do not see the men I spoke to in February but I recognise the look among the people queueing for tea, charging their phones and playing Connect Four and cards: mostly young, strikingly friendly, tracksuited, and, despite the freezing rain, often flip-flopped.

Gess shakes her head. 'They wear flip-flops because if their shoes get wet they will never dry,' she says.

★

'I have good reasons,' says a 26-year-old taxi driver and singer from Sudan, who prefers not to give his name. A tall, charismatic man, he says his protest song about the military regime in Khartoum provoked police raids on his home.

'In France and Italy, Africans like us cannot have good lives. People move away from you on the bus. The UK is not like this – I have my brother there and he says come, it is better. He is younger and he wants me to look after him, so I must go as fast as possible.'

In between talking to me, he deals with questions and conversations from a group of people who seem to rely on him for answers and solutions. His manner is both fatherly and managerial as he stoops, chides and directs men and youths who are less organised or confident.

When I ask about their families and contact with home, the English graduate says he is not here at all. 'I don't tell my mother I'm in the Jungle. I tell her I am in a flat. If you understand how language affects people, you don't want your mother to worry and get ill.'

Many of the people now huddling under tarpaulins, as the rain refuses to slacken and the police trudge back to their vans, are 'living in flats', he says.

Before I even pose the why-Britain question, a 17-year-old Afghan, who has been playing obsessively since we arrived, cries, 'Cricket! Cricket for England!'

He is a right-arm-over-the-blue-plastic-wicket fast bowler and an all-rounder, judging by his controlled and fierce cover drives. At close of play, he stows the equipment carefully in the charity's van.

The police have had at least one success – a young Sudanese boy has lost his tent. The singer taxi driver, who suddenly looks doubly tall, immediately offers the lad a place in his. 'Two in one tent!' he grimaces, 'Eee!'

★

Standing alone, the rain soaking his hat and trousers, is a young Sudanese web designer with a Masters in information technology. He has only been here a couple of days, he says, and you can see the wariness with which he eyes the groups of established men.

'My primary reason is language. To start in a new country with nothing is impossible if you don't have the language. I have family in England – not first-line family. But when I get there I will contact them and they will help.'

He does not look sure of this. He does not look sure of anything as he talks about hope and destiny, and the light dies towards dark. The volunteers pack away the generators and phone-charging boards.

'Do you know much about life in England?' I ask.

'I don't know much about it,' he says, quietly, and you feel instinctively that he cannot bear to look closely. 'I have to get there for my family,' he says, and then explains he has 'a Dublin'.

Because his fingerprints and photo were taken in Romania, he explains, he will be sent back there if he is picked up, unless he reaches Britain, which is no longer part of the Dublin agreement that provides for people to be returned to their country of European entry: Romania, in his case.

An older man is wearing a blue tarpaulin as a hooded cloak. He has a wide, kind face. You could cast him as Shepherd in a dystopian nativity play. We have a very English conversation about the weather. 'It always rains here?' he says, as if incredulous.

'It rains a lot in the north and west,' I say. 'Because we're near the sea.'

'In the north and west?' he says. 'Near the sea. Because this is nature?'

'Yes,' I say, 'For the sun you want to be in the south and east!' And as I say it, the appalling crassness of this statement strikes me. Along with civil war, droughts and floods are flaying his homeland, 3,000 miles south-east of us.

He sees my awkwardness and embarrassment in an instant. 'God makes some people rich, some people poor, but we can all hope. We can be strong,' he says, reassuringly.

Shivering there in the mud I have the sensation of a country floating near here, over the roofs and beyond the sand dunes, just over the water from Blériot Plage. It is a kind country, a fair country, a generous and welcoming country. It is a nation with a glorious history inhabited by people who understand, who are not racist, who care what happens to strangers, who defend the weak and help the needy.

This is a nation gilded in the sunlight of *Midsomer Murders*, a once-great nation which gave a mighty language to people whose tongues are not spoken around the globe; a nation which minded about schools and games, and courts and hospitals, about justice and fairness, a nation which left versions of its stories, its institutions and its ideals, its sports and its customs in the countries it colonised and ruled, and left versions of its highest beliefs and aspirations, too, in a hundred million minds and a hundred million families.

It is a wild and skewed and partial dream, but it is a dream with beauty in it, and magnificence, and inspiration, uncompromised by fact or history, with every doubt and detail driven out of it by the flood of mighty hope on which it rides. You can see why nothing these people might have heard about what it is actually like to be a refugee in Britain can possibly deter them.

The distribution is done, the day over and Gess exhausted. When she lets herself think about what is happening here, when I ask her to think about it, she exudes a bone-deep tiredness. By her pallor, her stare and her listlessness, any doctor or therapist would diagnose her with traumatic stress before she had even begun to talk.

'The human brain can only take so much,' she says. 'So much death. So much stress and death and worry. You are only thinking about the people. It gets worse, so you stay to help, and your phone rings all the time. You don't think about the people you have helped, only the ones you haven't. The things you didn't have time to do.'

This is the change the year has wrought. Britain remains as alluring as ever, the hope it offers is undiminished, but with weather deteriorating and police sweeps intensifying, the damage to minds and bodies is palpable.

There is a sick man in Unicorn camp; he has medication but his condition is worsening. Gess rings around her contacts. Messages come back – there is no bed for him, we have no space, sorry, sorry...

Across the sea, a British chancellor is relying on a surge of migrant labour to fill 1.2 million job vacancies. 'Only higher-than-expected immigration adds materially to prospects for potential output growth over the coming five years,' according to the Office for Budget Responsibility.

You read that and re-read it and the dissonance is dizzying. We are relying on immigration to save our economy and we are doing everything we can to deter immigration. Britain has a critical shortage of ICT graduates. No British politician, I tell myself, will come here to explain to the Information and Communications Technology graduate that he is the wrong kind of solution to our problems, essentially because he looks like the wrong kind of 'migrant', and because he is standing in the mud with other people who look like they may be the wrong kind of migrant, too. The cost of the asylum system at this point, 2022–23, is £3.6 billion. The national debt will reach £2.8 trillion in 2025.

Nevertheless, Britannia remains resolved to spend ever more money, energy and political willpower on breaking the spirits of people who long to give her everything they have. And so it is that every nightmare, every hunger pang, every cough and shiver and desperate thought in the wastes of Calais tonight can be counted a British victory, if not quite the kind you would want to see beneath the Union Jack.

The Politician vs the Volunteer

I was wrong about British politicians not coming to Calais, but not about what they would or would not say on seeing the conditions here, on meeting the people who live in this brutal squalor, and those who try to help.

In January 2023, a Home Affairs committee of the British government visits Calais 'to examine the current situation with Channel crossings in small boats', it reports. One of the members of the committee is the Member of Parliament for Ashfield, Lee Anderson, who is appointed deputy chair of the Conservative party the following month. Anderson is a fascinating figure, the son of a coal miner who followed his father into the pits where he worked for ten years before becoming a volunteer, then an employee, at the Citizens Advice Bureau. He worked in hostels for homeless people who were leaving the care system. He became a Labour councillor before defecting to the Conservative party and becoming an MP in 2019. His defection came after he was suspended from his branch of the Labour party for organising the dumping of boulders intended to block members of the travelling community from setting up a campsite.

Anderson is a large man with short white hair, a pouched face and an expression balanced between calculating and pugnacious. His Nottinghamshire accent and his plain speaking recall Arthur Scargill, the leader of the National Union of

Mineworkers in the 1980s, whom Anderson cites as an early influence, along with Dennis Skinner, Michael Foot and Tony Benn. The young Anderson was a member of the National Union of Mineworkers (NUM); he now locates himself as a right-wing populist, with a creed of tell-it-how-you-see-it, we-want-our-country-back.

Unusually for a British politician, and perhaps especially for one who has travelled from the socialist left to the hard right, Anderson's primary quality appears to be authenticity. Like the unabashed Skinner, like the impassioned Scargill, Anderson does not seem to have to decide what he thinks – or what might be appropriate to say about what he thinks, or how he thinks – before he speaks. He sounds guileless because he does not seem to measure his words against how they might sound or the positioning of his party.

Whatever you think of his views, this robustness is striking. In the same way that Donald Trump draws and engrosses the world's gaze – a gaze glazed by the mundanity and inanity of the PR-polished, on-message, let-me-be-very-clear political world – Anderson projects an almost childlike charisma. He looks like one of the bigger kids in the playground, the one who could sway the mob either way. You do not quite know what he is going to say next, only that it will come out with conviction, which makes his interviewers treat him as if he is both interesting and frightening.

Anderson's visit to Calais is remarkable in that he manages to make a public figure of himself and to make the situation in Calais markedly worse, and the divisions over immigration in Britain deeper, in the space of two days.

Before he reaches the wastelands, Anderson films himself and an aide on a coach. Both seem excited to hear that the police have just swept the camp. 'They must have known we were coming ... that's what happens when the Red Wall comes to Northern France!'

At the Old Lidl shanty-camp, Anderson is clearly in sympathy with the people living in the tents and bushes. It is bitterly cold, he says, and he feels sorry for them. At a second stop he films himself having just talked to Care4Calais volunteers. One of the volunteers, when challenged about her work, returned the challenge, he says, asking him if Britain did not owe something to the refugees and migrants, having colonised their countries during the period of the British Empire. Anderson ridicules this: 'When she said that she lost the argument, really.'

He goes on to repeat his sympathy for the people living in the squalid desolation. He can see they have nothing, but, he concludes, 'What they do have is hope, and this charity, they may be well-intentioned, but they're giving them hope.'

Anderson also says he has challenged the charity about people throwing away their documents before they reach Britain, and asked if Care4Calais tells people not to cross the sea. He claims the charity does not do this.

Thus far, thus fair enough. He has been to the sites, met some of the people involved, listened to them, and formed or reinforced his own opinions. It is what happens next that is sinister.

On his return to Britain, Anderson takes to social media, the newspapers and GB News to denounce Care4Calais and charities like them.

'They are just as bad as the people smugglers,' he says. He goes further, saying they act as a magnet for migrants, and telling GB News he had repeatedly heard the phrase 'El Dorado' – from the police, and, he says, from the people hoping to cross the Channel.

El Dorado, he says, is how these people see Britain. With the heavy plain speaking that a man of the people reserves for foreign languages, he says he believes the phrase means 'city of gold', and that he heard it repeatedly from police and people he calls 'migrants'. (The people he met were overwhelmingly Sudanese, who have a 99 per cent grant rate for asylum at initial decision, so the accurate description would be 'refugees'.)

No one he spoke to, he says, mentioned fleeing war or persecution; all, he said, wanted to go to 'El Dorado', to Britain, for a better life. You have to rewatch the recordings Anderson made in Calais and the interviews he gives afterwards for the oddity to appear. Where does the phrase 'El Dorado' come from, and when does he hear it? Does anyone in the illegal settlements actually say it? Watching his films and reading his posts repeatedly, I start to doubt his account. If anyone does say that Britain is 'El Dorado', why does he not report it when he hears it? There he is, in the two wastelands he visits, and both times he is quoting what he has seen and heard. Then there he is at the Calais seafront on his way home after the visits, saying he is 'furious' and 'foaming' at what the charity is doing, and that Care4Calais is part of the problem. Then he is back in his constituency, tired, the next morning, but only in this clip does he mention the phrase 'El Dorado'. Why?

It matters, because 'El Dorado' is the centrepiece of the interview he gives to GB News. It is the pearl of his 'findings' in Calais, posted on social media. Perhaps the French police say it to him – he says they did, and you can well imagine them using the shorthand. The view in Calais, repeatedly expressed by the authorities there, is that it is Britain's benefits system, and the impression the refugees have of the country, which lures them.

'El Dorado' is not a phrase any of the refugees I have interviewed ever used. The words clash with what they do say and do know of the United Kingdom. 'It is better, it is fairer, you can have a better life there, British people are not racist, my brother says it is better, I speak English.' You hear all these, but you do not hear colourful metaphors for a land of gold and free money. My guess is, Anderson takes 'El Dorado' from the shorthand of the police or the Calais authorities, puts it into the mouths of the people at Old Lidl and other shanty camps, and then sends it out into the indignation bubble, to watch it multiply. It is such a simple, powerful slogan, and I believe it is a lie.

I email Clare Moseley of Care4Calais and ask, 'Have you ever heard one of the rough sleepers refer to Britain as "El Dorado"? I think Anderson made it up.'

Her reply comes swiftly:

'I thought exactly the same thing. A refugee would never say that in a million years. And I've met thousands.'

Anderson's visit to Calais is a great success for him. GB News offers him his own show, 'Lee Anderson's Real World'. Anderson's actions also alter the behaviour of the French authorities and the police, and changes what the police do to the volunteers. In the aftermath of the visit, I interview Gess online. She looks better, pale and exhausted but better. She is taking three days off, her first for months.

She says that two of Care4Calais' team leaders have quit: 'They left from one day to the other so we've been working very hard.'

'How are the refugees?' I ask.

'There are less than before. I'm very surprised, there's not too many people right now. Maybe 400–500 in the Jungle. Some people told me it became very hard to get from Libya to Italy. The boats are very expensive and the police are extremely bad. So if less people reach Italy, less people reach Calais. And the situation in the UK is not helpful at all.'

The situation to which she refers includes more talk of deporting people to Rwanda; more small boat crossings; Cabinet ministers claiming that arrivals by sea should have 'no rights'; government sources threatening to pull out of the European Convention on Human Rights rather than back down over the Nationality and Borders Bill, which denies people the right to claim asylum. The mood in Britain appears to be an ugly ferment of hostility, division and anger.

During this period, the Immigration Minister, Robert Jenrick, visits Dover. At a reception centre for unaccompanied children seeking asylum, Jenrick sees murals of Disney characters painted on the walls, a small effort to make the place feel less threatening to children. Jenrick orders the murals be painted over. They are, he is reported to have felt, 'too welcoming'. Horrified staff resist the order but Jenrick's office sends in contractors to efface the pictures.

There are several extraordinary characters in this story, including Lee Anderson and Suella Braverman, but Jenrick, who owns two houses in London worth well over £2 million each, and a substantial grade one listed country manor house, and charges taxpayers over £2,000 a month to maintain a fourth house in his constituency, catches the eye. The effacement of the murals suggests Robert Jenrick struggles to see the least fortunate and the most vulnerable, unaccompanied child refugees – *children who have crossed the Channel on small boats without parents or guardians* – as members of his own species. But when you watch him giving a thoughtful interview to the BBC's Newscast programme, he comes across as sincere in a way neither Anderson or Braverman appear to be; while they both appear intoxicated by themselves, Jenrick seems genuinely worried by what he perceives as a much wider problem than the small boats. He worries about housing, about lack of integration, about communities 'living parallel lives'. You can see why he has been appointed to power. He is quick, clear and apparently truthful. 'Very large numbers of people coming into the country make it difficult for us to build the united country we all want to see,' he says.

Leaving aside the question of what sort of country 'we all want to see' – does he mean a white country? – the wriggle here is the 'very large numbers', and whether they are, objectively, bad or good news.

In 2023, net migration in the year to June was 672,000. Those who came in small boats numbered 29,000: just 4 per cent. This visible, demonised 4 per cent are treated as the whole story by the government, the commentators and the press. This 4 per cent from the Channel are made to carry all the responsibility, the anguish, the worry and the ire which attaches to 672,000 *legal* immigrants, immigrants without whom many of our businesses and public services could not function, as the Chancellor of the Exchequer admits.

Having looked hard at Britain's housing, communities and migration policy, Robert Jenrick has concluded, he tells his BBC interviewers, that 'If you want to fix this, like Australia did and like Greece has done more recently, you have to accept that you've got to do some very tough things.'

In Australia's case, that meant pushing boats out of Australian waters and off-shoring their passengers to holding centres on islands, described by the International Criminal Court as 'cruel, inhuman, degrading treatment', illegal under international law.

In the case of Greece, these 'very tough things' have included beatings by police and coastguards, normalised pushbacks, towing vessels away, causing capsizes and deaths, swamping dinghies with the wakes of border-patrol craft, pointing guns at refugees, assaults by masked security forces, strip searches, detentions, abuse, forcible transfers to Turkish waters and marooning people on life rafts, according to multiple accounts collated by the charity Médecins Sans Frontières.

It is not clear how far along this path to dirty warfare against desperate people Robert Jenrick would be prepared to go, but his admiration for Australian and Greek policies certainly explains why he took against the murals in a reception centre for children. A hostile environment has to start somewhere, after all.

★

Gess says the hostility in Britain – the reported hostility at least – is not lost on the rough sleepers of Calais.

'They're reading newspapers every day, so they're very updated on the situation. People still cross. A couple of nights ago a lot of boats reached UK, so the situation there doesn't stop it. People who weren't sure if they were going to go to the UK, maybe they go somewhere else. But people who come with the idea of going to the UK – they're still going to go.'

I ask about the effect of the visit by the Home Affairs committee.

'Lee Anderson came over to Calais and he was horrible to refugees, to charities, to everybody. After he came down to Calais the police came harder than before, more to us than them, but with us they became harder – more control, more harsh, more checking. An article in an English newspaper came out very insulting to all of us, saying we help immigrants to cross the Channel – it was very offensive. They wrote that the volunteers were at the beach blocking the police and helping people to cross. It's absolutely *wrong*. Nobody does this. The only thing that happens is that the Utopia charity goes to the beach with coffee and tea waiting for people to come back, to stop them dying of cold. They go there with blankets and tea and coffee to make sure they don't die of cold!'

'Did Anderson's visit really change the way the police treat you?' I press her.

'Yes. The police stop you all the time, try to find something wrong with the vehicle, something wrong with you, they ask a lot of questions, check documents. They try to find a reason to send the English volunteers back to England. They can't do that much to me, sometimes they are polite, sometimes they are extremely rude – "Fucking Italian", this is the words they use. It depends why they stop you, on the mood they have that day, if they're new, if they've been here long.'

'That must be frightening?'

'They don't have respect. There are rules even for police, and if you let them know they can't do this, everybody has the same reaction. They touch their badge and say, "I'm police, I can do anything." You must know the law – or they literally smash your head. It's on you. If you know what you're doing and you know your rights, then you can win. You say, "I can call the lawyer", and they go back.'

'What is your relationship like with the people of Calais? What is the situation in the town?' I ask.

Gess looks solemn and wan but she sounds resolute.

'We start to do a lot of protests in Calais with French people, and that makes me feel we're fighting now, not just watching. On Sunday we did a big commemoration which we do every year on the borders – they did it yesterday in Ventimiglia. We do a commemoration for all the people who die on the borders. A hundred people came from all of France, Netherlands, Germany, Paris. The majority were volunteers, people who help people at the borders, where people don't care about these things. We walked to the theatre and to the small park in the centre, and we read some words of a guy who lost his brother. He wrote this sort of letter, and it was very touching. He wrote as if he was the dead guy. It was very sad and very, very intense. We write all the names of people who died here from 2014 to now. Whenever somebody dies at the border, we do a commemoration in the park. It's important that you make it human because their family is not here, so somebody needs to remember them and give them a face. It is important. They are people.'

'Almost 400 names on that piece of paper?' I ask. 'As many people as you're looking after, you're commemorating?'

'Yes. Sometimes it's depressing – you think why are we doing this? Nothing changes, nobody cares, you talk with journalists, and nothing changes and you feel like everything we do is not helpful. At the same time it is important that we are there, because if we are not there, who is going to be there for them? Our presence keeps them alive, so it's important. We give them hope.'

'And the people of Calais? How do they treat you?'

'Some of the people of Calais support us, some no. They never see me, I'm always in the Jungle or in the warehouse.'

'Where are you living?'

'Sometimes in the squat, sometimes in a caravan. I think I'm leaving in March. I've been here two years. I will go to work a little bit in Spain, just work in a hostel maybe, something easy. I need a really big break. Something very easy and chill, so I can rest a little bit. Actually, it's been three years. I was in Ventimiglia for a year. I experience different stuff every day – because I don't just do what Care4Calais do, I do a lot of extra, taking care of people's mental health, especially.'

'What does that involve?'

'One of my friends tried to kill himself. Now he is in the UK, I hope now he's fine. I've been taking care of him a lot. There was a guy, nobody knew why but he was arrested for no reason. He was taken off the street and he was in prison six months, and when he was let free he became extremely paranoid. So he hid somewhere far away from all the other people. He never moved. He was not going to distributions, not going to the church, to the other charities, not even to pick up food. He was very isolated and paranoid in case he got taken to prison again. So slowly, slowly my friend introduced me to him. Very slowly, until he trusted me so I could take care of him, bring him clothes, bring him food, keep him company. He was from Sudan.'

'I never ask personal questions if they don't want to talk to me about it,' Gess continues. 'Especially people with mental disorders, I never ask questions. It's very easy to see. If someone hides himself, if he doesn't see people, if he lives alone.'

'Do you feel you've made a difference?'

'I know I've made a difference to some people for sure. Because they've told me. So I'm sure about that. I did my best. Some people told me. When I get very down there's this amazing woman at Secours Catholique and I speak with her and she's like, "Ok, we can't change the world, we can't change everything, *but* imagine the impact we have on these people. Imagine if we weren't here." She tells me, "You do a lot, you work 24 hours a day, imagine if you weren't here." What we're doing is important for people. We're not going to change the situation but it's important for the people living here. So according to her we changed something.'

'But *why* do you do it?'

'Because I'm like this. This is me. I got lost a little bit here and there and I took the wrong way, but then I found it again. But my head is full right now. I need a break and then I can make a plan. I just need to go and rest a little bit. Three years is a long time, and I've never processed what I've been through. I've been through a lot here and lost a lot of people. And a lot of the pain in the night – I don't have time to elaborate on it – and because I was always busy. You need to be always 100 per cent for the guys and be happy, so you just keep going and keep going and you ignore whatever happens to you because you need to be strong for them. To be honest, I would like to come back to Calais as an independent.'

'But what drives you to keep doing it? To keep helping people?'

'I think it's unfair that white Europeans can go everywhere. These people are running away from starvation and war – what's the difference between us and them? We are human beings, all of us. It's not fair. I must help people. I stand for the most fragile. When I see injustice, I get crazy and I need to change it. I need to do something.'

★

85

Gess's Italian accent and emphasis mean her conclusion does not sound the way it would from a native English speaker. We might emphasise the *do* (we must act) or the *something* (howsoever we can). Italian stresses the penultimate syllable, so she says, I need to do *some*thing. It seems to speak exactly of what she does and why. There in Calais, between the Continent and the sea, between the despair they have left and the hope that draws them, these men have fallen as if into a crevice, into the wastelands. They are some people, somewhere, in some trouble. To support them and care for them is beyond unfashionable. It is to be despised, to be bullied, to be harassed, to be overlooked, to be unpaid, to be slandered and to be picked on.

What makes the work Gess does especially vital to her, it seems, is that she knows, and the people she is helping know, that this is not necessarily the worst of it. This is just one stop on the trail, and the trail stretches out for years ahead, assuming you survive the crossing.

Across the water, a man has died at the Manston processing centre in Kent, where violence, squalor, overcrowding and outbreaks of scabies and diphtheria left its inspector, David Neal, the then Independent Chief Inspector of Borders and Immigration, 'speechless'.

A far-right extremist has attacked a reception centre at Dover.

One Home Secretary, Priti Patel, has tried and failed to off-shore asylum claimants to Rwanda, but Rwanda has not gone away, and everybody in the wastelands knows it.

Patel's successor, Suella Braverman, signs away £63 million to this region to pay for more police, more technology and more patrols on the beaches. Any of the people on the Channel coast who succeed in crossing will join the 41,000 people who crossed this year. Any who claim asylum will join a processing queue that is 103,000 people long at the end of June 2022.

The UK Home Office reports it has processed just 4 per cent of last year's claims, granting refugee or similar status in 85 per cent of cases.

The British political temperature around this issue is as high as the numbers of claims granted are low. The Migration Observatory at the University of Oxford points out that when adjusted for population size, the UK ranks 18th in Europe for granting protection, accepting two asylum seekers per 10,000 of the population.

Statistically, then, the problem is not the legitimacy of claims or the numbers taken in. The problems are the numbers waiting in hotels, reception centres and temporary accommodation, and the extraordinary cost of the entire system to the British taxpayer: over £2.1 billion in 2022, which rises to £4.7 billion in 2024, according to the National Audit Office. The price of the queue is running at over a million pounds a day. The government and Prime Minister appear to be sinking under their inability to do anything about the boats or the hotel backlog, and the opposition Labour Party are not offering any particular solutions: all they have to do, they figure, is wait.

And then, in the middle of this mess, there emerges a new idea. A solution. A symbol. A novel way of addressing the whole problem. A deterrent and a cost-cutter, something that not even the courts can stop. A show of business-like tough-mindedness, seriousness and competence: the British government is going to rent a boat. The British government is going to fill this boat with asylum seekers, relieving the cost, deterring the crossings, and, if all goes well, proving that boats are the answer to boats. We could have several ships full of asylum seekers. We could have a fleet! The government charters the first vessel. It's called *Bibby Stockholm*.

7

The Boat

We drive at night, the motorways all but empty for miles and miles, England hot and silent in the darkness. We sleep in the car at a service station near Exeter, wake to a yellow day warming, and come down into Falmouth through the long green lanes. The Home Office's 'accommodation barge', *Bibby Stockholm*, is being refitted in Falmouth port. There is a rumour that the *Bibby* might be moving today, out of dry dock in Falmouth and on to Portland, where she is to be berthed and crewed with people from the asylum claims queue. I approach the police guards at the port gate.

'Can I help you?'

'Yes! I would like a tour of the *Bibby Stockholm*, please.'

They start laughing.

'I'm afraid we can't do that for you.'

I explain that I am down here to write about the boat and that I will be poking around a lot, with no wish to alarm anyone. The police are cordial. There have already been protests here about the boat. They say they do not know when she will be moving on. The map of the port on the wall behind them shows her berth.

At the Falmouth Hotel a duty manager takes to my partner, Esther, to whom people are immediately drawn. Esther has never worked on a reporting team before, but I have kidnapped her for this mission. 'It will be fun! You'll see!' I promised, before driving her for ten hours and putting her up in the passenger seat at the service station.

'Are you on holiday?' the manager asks.

I explain that we're writing about *Bibby Stockholm*, and the manager starts talking to Esther about the boat.

'The word is the rooms are nice but the hull is rotten,' the manager says.

The *hull* is rotten? The bit of a boat that makes a boat a boat is *rotten*?

'Yes, that's what the people working on the boat are saying. The steel is worn out.'

The symbol of the government's new grip on the asylum backlog is sitting in a dry dock below the cliff road. We park and get out, and there she is. *Bibby Stockholm* is a peculiar structure, a giant dirty-pink portacabin with a sagging roof and small windows, like a primitive prison, space turned tightly in on itself. It is not just that she is ugly or utterly charmless. She seems sinister.

We count windows and do the sums. The government are saying they will put 500 people in this vessel, but only 200 of them are going to have windows, we reckon.

'Bunk beds?' Esther guesses. She speaks with two men in a van who are camping here, above the barge, as an act of protest. 'They're calling her the Bibby Stockholm Syndrome,' she says.

'Where are the fire escapes?' we ask each other. There are no fire escapes. Indeed, the only exits are on one side of the vessel. If your cabin is on the other side and the thing catches fire, your only option is to jump out of the window into the sea. We make sketches, take photographs and try to work out how the *Bibby* is supposed to function. It does not seem to have any power of its own – are they going to plug it into the mains? Into generators?

There are a lot of dock workers coming and going, their overalls marked A&P, the company which owns the dry docks and is refitting the vessel. *Bibby* is owned by Bibby Marine (a Liverpool shipping company which made its first money in the slave trade) and chartered to Corporate Travel Management (CTM), an Australian outsourcing company, and will be spoken for by Landry and Kling, a PR-friendly ship-sourcing duo who will give interviews about their admirably feminist company and their care for refugees.

Co-founder Joyce Landry will describe the boat as 'actually quite lovely', and lie about why it is currently stuck in Falmouth. She will claim that the delay is due to 'the weather gods', while Esther and I watch work on the hull going on around the clock.

It turns out that CTM got the contract for the *Bibby* without having to compete for it, because they already had a contract for providing cars, flights and accommodation for the government, allowing the *Bibby* to be slipped onto the bill. CTM have a £1.6 billon pound contract to run this barge, and presumably others like it, for two years, extendable.

We go into town and start asking around. Where would the dock workers drink? The place to watch out for, we are told, is the Arwenack Club, a locals' bar.

On the main street, overlooking the harbour through huge windows, the Arwenack was formerly the Royal British Legion Club. On the walls are ships' crests, the plaques like battle honours which ships present to ports on their first visits, and a poem in praise of the Royal Fleet Auxiliary, two of whose huge ships dominate the harbour. 'Oh I *love* it!' Esther whispers.

We meet water gypsies who grew up on boats, live on boats, couch-surf on boats, and dockers, and people whose mates are dockers. Becca, a chef, introduces us to Luke, who looks like a young Cornish pirate, and Vinny, who is a Cornish pirate. I hire Luke to take us seagoing, to look at *Bibby* from the water.

Nobody here has anything against asylum seekers or refugees. They are as curious and sceptical about the *Bibby Stockholm* as we are.

'Bibby's a cursed ship,' a man tells me. 'There were abusive incidents on her before.'

In Jacob's Ladder, a bar on the top of the hill where sea people drink, Esther leads half the staff and customers in karaoke while I talk with two men who have been in the yard with the *Bibby* all day.

'The hull has to be three millimetres thick, minimum,' says one. 'When they scanned it they found it wasn't, so they've had to replace whole sections. They're replacing them with five-millimetre plates. That ain't cheap.'

'When A&P inspected it, they found the water tanks were rotten – they needed to be blasted out,' says the man's friend. 'The people running the barge said *Can't we just go anyway?* A&P said no. Without safe tanks, it fails the inspection. That's two more weeks at a million pounds a week.'

These are skilled, steady men who cannot give their names. I put their claims to the Home Office, and to the port authorities in Falmouth. No denials are forthcoming. The authorities respond with silence on the attempt to move with the tanks unfinished, and 'cannot confirm or deny' the rotten steel.

The strange thing is, the harder we look, the more people we speak to about what is happening here, the more clearly the true story of the *Bibby Stockholm* emerges, the more and the deeper my affection and respect grows – for Falmouth, and for this England.

I like the police and their sense of humour, guarding the *Bibby's* gates. I admire the workers – around-the-clock really means that here, and at half past three on a Sunday night/ Monday morning, they are still at it, three separate work gangs going at the hull. Amidships starboard they are banging a plate into place with a big hammer, on the starboard quarter they are welding, and under the bow a third party are working with an angle grinder.

I like and admire Jimmy in his van up above the barge, sleeping in a bag, bunking up with his dog, keeping up a kind of karmic protest in the name of people he has never met who will be consigned to the barge. When I wake Jimmy late on a sunny morning, he stretches an arm out of his sleeping bag, puts the coffee on and begins a quiet and thoughtful discussion about the difference between xenophobia and localism.

'Localism is the issue here,' he says. 'It's not about dislike or fear of migrants or refugees or foreigners. It's about fear for your place in your local community, for what's happening to that community.'

Jimmy explains that protests against migrants are an expression of despair at house prices driven mad by second homes and holiday lets, at stuttering public services. Anti-migrant demonstrations are driven by fear of what happens to Cornish children if the schools are no good, the health service overloaded, the universities too expensive, the jobs far away.

And yet there is work here, and there could be much more.

'The UK government is offering £1.6 million as a competitive tender open to all the ports of the UK to upgrade infrastructure,' says Miles Carden, CEO of Falmouth Port, when I call him. Not each, he clarifies – £1.6 million between them.

'We are going to have huge windfarms offshore, which we are going to rely on for our energy, and the vessels which build and service them will be hybrids, and they'll need to be charged up, crewed and maintained. £1.6 million is not even *close* to enough. £1.6 billion would be more like it.'

If this was Holland, he speculates, the money would already have been paid and work on the charging points and berths started.

There is nothing like a port visit to expose the bones of strategic competition. Britain's oldest rivals at sea, the Dutch, French and Spanish, are just beyond the horizons of the South Coast. They know the big bucks are made offshore, and they know how to build and run the ships and turbines that will land them. The money, the industry and governmental head-space devoted to the *Bibby* and her context are costing the country valuable funds, and invaluable concentration on matters of much more importance, is Miles Carden's point.

Luke Arch has a 'deflatable': a small boat named *Orca* which needs lots of pumping-up to stay afloat, but is otherwise excellent, he says, small, fast and strong. I hire Luke, buy life jackets, and Luke takes Esther and me to sea. He grins at the possibility of *Orca* sinking. 'Shouldn't do. I've been on the water since I was four.'

We set out across Falmouth harbour, through the maze of moored yachts, buzzing past the pilot vessels and out to the huge Royal Fleet Auxiliary supply ships. Their grey hulls loom giant above us. Down channel with a following sea we go, and around to the mouth of the dry dock, where we photograph *Bibby* from the water. Back up the harbour we batter into the flow of the Fal, the wind and the tide, the little engine fighting us into the short waves, the water dashing over the bow, *Orca* battling on as her tube deflates no matter how hard we pump. The sea is coming in from ahead of us, over the tube and over Esther in gouts, and the sea is coming from behind us, up from the stern in sloppy surges. We seem as much in the water as on it. I am steering. All I can do is keep the throttle open as much as possible, driving into the waves, slackening slightly at the top of each big one, trying not to bash us too hard in the trough, trying not to take in too much more water. The water keeps coming. Luke pumps, I throttle, and the tube is emptying, flaccid, grey and useless. We are all soaked and shivering, adrenaline fighting cold.

'It's not connected!' Esther cries, jamming the pump's nozzle into a valve and we all yell with rueful glee – and now the tube is inflating and all will be well. The three of us drifting out of Falmouth harbour under the vast steel wall of the navy supply ship, wearing our bright-orange jackets, would have been bad but probably not fatal. It is midsummer, there are boats around. Someone would have spotted us, surely. And all the same, the cold, deep sea is just there, on an inflatable, waiting for you on the other side of a softening tube.

Carrick Roads, the estuary of the Fal, Helford and Penryn rivers, is a splay of creeks and anchorages. Low green peninsulas and headlands slope down to inlets and reaches. The whole panorama shifts with clear young sea light and old summer land light, dimming and brightening with the passage of high clouds overhead. We go on up the river to where the tugs are moored. One of them may be used to move the *Bibby Stockholm* to Portland, but we do not know when. The pace of work in the dry dock is relentless, with the costs obviously spiralling and the political pressure to deliver this 'solution' constant.

By the standards of British seaside towns, some of which, like Scarborough, Blackpool, Minehead and Weston-super-Mare hold the country's deepest pockets of deprivation, Falmouth is a happy place. There are jobs in the port, in the docks, in the hotels and bars; there is the university, the marine school, the Maritime museum; there is still a vibrant local newspaper, the *Falmouth Packet*; there are tides of tourists, travellers and visitors arriving by land and sea.

Our new friend, Becca, working as a chef, tells us she left her upbringing in Somerset, and will never go back. 'I love Falmouth! The best thing about Bridgwater is the road out of it,' she laughs. Luke says he has never been out of Cornwall. I recruit both of them, and Jimmy in his van above the docks: when *Bibby* moves they will call me and I will ensure that the photographer, Harry Mitchell, is in Portland to catch her.

On the quay we run into the author Adam Nicolson and the broadcaster David Dimbleby, who seem to be holidaying on David's yacht. Adam looks foolishly happy in his life jacket. A polymath and a writer of some of Britain's most beautiful prose, he is in holiday mood, laughing and probing. 'What are you doing here?' David looks as wintery as the commander of a destroyer. 'I like him because he's a writer,' he says, nodding at Adam. 'He likes me because I'm on television.' Adam giggles. Oh, this *is* England, I think, you couldn't ask for more, and David Dimbleby to present it.

And just around the corner, all day and all night, they are working on this strange hybrid half-ship thing, this bizarre compilation of barge and bunker, prison and pledge. I keep being struck by how expert Britain is, by how competent the country can be. We meet a crew who are working on a power connector between England and Morocco, a cable which will run along the continental shelf, avoiding the deeps of the Bay of Biscay, to bring solar and wind power from the Moroccan Sahara to the National Grid.

It makes you want to cheer – here comes the future, from the desert to Devon and Cornwall! From 1688 to 1850 the Falmouth packet ships brought all the world's information to Britain and landed it here, entrusting the doings of the day and the shape of the future to this town's harbour, the palm of the county's hand, outstretched to the Atlantic. The *Bibby* is the latest in a long line of historic Falmouth-fated ships. In October 1836 the *Beagle* came into Carrick Roads and Charles Darwin disembarked, unimpressed:

> After a tolerably short passage, but with some very heavy weather, we came to an anchor at Falmouth. To my surprise and shame, I confess the first sight of the shores of England inspired me with no warmer feelings than if it had been a mud-walled Portuguese settlement. The same night (and a dreadfully stormy one it was), I started by the Mail for Shrewsbury.

Just like that, the whole of the world changes. A person steps off a ship and goes ashore and nothing will be the same again. Imagine the human potential among all those men, women and children who have come ashore in Dover and on the Kent coast. Imagine the riches. Thanks to that disembarking passenger of 1836, superstition, ignorance and the skewed power of the Church will be driven backwards. Britain as a country and humanity as a species will know more, think more, find more, be more. And we're at it again, tonight in Falmouth, trying something new, something against the orthodoxy, something radical, something widely opposed. Only this time, it is not light we are pursuing, or enlightenment, or understanding. This time we are hammering and welding and grinding and inspecting and doing everything we can to make a monster.

Late at night, I stand on the cliff road, binoculars focused on the *Bibby Stockholm*. Staring in through her dark cabin windows I can see the shapes of chairs and desks within, illuminated by lights in her corridors. You half expect to see the shadows of men with their small bags, unpacking, making their own corners in the space they are given. You can smell them, as the numbers grow, and the space shrinks, and you can almost hear them. You can hear them all night long.

She is a prison, alright. A prison with dodgy water tanks, inadequate fire safety, too few ways to get off, no life rafts, sagging roof, no air-conditioning – she is perfect, I realise, for the purpose for which she is intended. Her first unwilling crews will suffer at every stage. They will suffer when they are notified they are going to be taken aboard, they will suffer when they get there, and they will suffer as long as they are cooped up there.

The press will report what the men go through, and the worse the better, the government must hope, so that the word will spread all the way across the sea to Calais, and back along the networks and trails, by phone and word of mouth, to who knows how far?

'The boat and Rwanda, the boat and Rwanda ...' the Home Secretary must be thinking – though the day we arrive in Falmouth the Court of Appeal rules against the Rwanda plan, judging that there is a significant risk that deportees could be returned to their home countries, and there face the mistreatment they have fled. The government is going to appeal to the Supreme Court. For now, British immigration policy, the pledge to 'stop the boats' and the answer to the asylum backlog is down there under high dock lights, being hit with hammers.

In mid-July the *Bibby Stockholm* moves to Portland, pulled up the coast by *Mercia*, one of Falmouth's tugs. Harry Mitchell photographs her being brought in for the *Financial Times* story I am writing. She looks like a brick on a long line; *Mercia* a tiny bath toy dragging her across the sunrise over a flat summer sea. GB News have their camera set up in the same spot.

In the days before *Bibby* moves, I take up temporary residence in Portland, a singular little England, an island which is not an island, thanks to the causeway, a feisty upthrust of rock, the stone on the end of the long sling of Chesil Beach. Walking along the shore on my first night, I meet two boys who claim they are fishing for coins with magnets. They are in their late teens and it all seems unlikely, like a weird dream of a bygone world, but there they are, casting little lines into the black sea at one in the morning. One of them jumps when I appear.

'Woah! Where have you come from?'

'Just round there.'

'Thought you'd come off the asylum boat.'

'I haven't! But I am writing about it... What's Portland like, then?'

'It's OK, yeah,' says one. 'As long as you're not caught with the wrong people.'

I ask about the heavy hand of security in Portland – the police, the cameras, the discreet and pervasive military-maritime air, which starts with nineteenth-century canons lying around and extends to the Navy helicopter which hovered high overhead this morning, surveying France and the Channel. And then there are the Second World War gun emplacements and guns, and the modern radars on the Verne hill, which survey all, and there are the rumours of a submarine base. I had barely got out of the car on Portland Bill when a man walking his dog told me there was a secret anchorage for nuclear submarines in Portland Deep, a pit in the seabed just off the headland.

The boys are not sure about this, but they are used to Portland's fortified horizons. 'Well there's the prison and the young offenders' prison,' says the second lad. 'And they do live firing on Chesil Beach.'

You might think it would feel oppressive to live beneath a horizon dominated by prisons, but Portland seems unbothered. By the happy chatter in the Jailhouse café, and the bustle in the canteen at the Young Offenders' prison, and by the friendly warder walking to work along the cliffs, who remarks on the beauty of the morning and his commute, people are grateful for the employment and activity incarceration brings.

★

And there is something odd about Portland. I can feel it as I explore the settlements, the cliffs, the monuments, the lookouts, the lighthouses, the seafronts. There is some strange ore, some compound of time, memory and tradition, glinting in the light of our modernity. In the Coastwatch lookout on Portland Bill, a retired naval officer describes the turbulent green-white water to the south of us. Between us and the Shambles sandbank, the east–west surge of the Channel's tides, switching direction every six hours, forms Portland Race, one of the most dangerous churns of currents and swells along England's coast. You can hear the race and the rush of the wind outside the lookout behind the storytelling burr of the Coastwatcher. He has a uniform, a radar, a rank and a role, just as he did in the navy. Now he is a volunteer.

'We watch every vessel that passes and we log their passage,' he says. 'We can easily see 15 miles through those!' He points to a gigantic pair of binoculars hydraulically fixed to the ceiling. 'And we've got radar and AIS too.'

His station reports to the Joint Rescue Coordination Centre in Fareham, the headquarters of the Coastguard. Like the RNLI, the National Coastwatch Institution is a highly professional organisation relying on voluntary labour and huge amateur and post-professional skill.

Like anyone else, any man from the *Bibby* could stroll by and press a button on the gate, and unless the volunteers are dealing with an emergency, one of them will usher you up the steps to the lookout and give you the tour of the charts, the instruments, the radar and the view, exactly as if you were a visiting inspector or King Charles himself. I cannot imagine an internee from the barge confidently approaching the wire and the cameras and pressing that bell button, though that is all it would take.

Through the windows you can see the cluster of buildings on the clifftop where Britain sets her true north. A 'magnetically

WE CAME BY SEA

clean' site, formerly run by the Admiralty and now in the hands of QinetiQ, a privatised arm of the defence establishment, it houses the 'acknowledged' compass needle, which is used to calibrate all British compasses and those of all UK-registered vessels.

Such a beautifully British arrangement, I think, as the watchers show me their realm. One officer talks to me about looking out for different sailing vessels – yachts, Bermudas and sloops – and how they log everything, including helicopters, and diverts into a brief history of Portland's role in submarine detection. Another officer, distinguished in white hair and spotless uniform, precisely and gently shows a new young volunteer how the AIS live map works, with the passing ships marked on it.

It does not matter where vessels come from, nor where they are bound, who is aboard, where they are flagged, or who owns them. These watchers look out for every one and meticulously record its passage, alert for any sign that it might need assistance. Extrapolate this line of dutifulness and painstaking public service from here to Westminster, and you would have a truly great Britain. We would *be* the country the people in the small boats imagine we are. *Set our true north here*, I think.

Curious Portland, scattered with derelict barracks, with sailors' graves, with plaques to men killed by misfired torpedoes, to once-upon-a-time helicopter bases. There are plaques to Portland stone, to disbanded fleets, to the sailing events of the London Olympics in 2012, to an entire family 'lost at Dunkirk'. People sit on benches and look out to sea, while others study bushes through binoculars – there are birdwatchers everywhere. Portland Bird Observatory on the Bill is one of the busiest and richest places for seeing, studying and ringing birds in the country. On one bench, there is a plaque identical to all the others, until you read it.

'Hiromi Kubota, Literati Painter, 1948–2048'

Someone in this miniature Britain has a wonderfully British sense of humour. Perhaps this odd place *is* our acknowledged needle, Britain's compass setting.

Even in high summer you can feel the shadow of our national soul here, too. A large slice of Portland's population is in the bottom 10 per cent of deprived areas of Britain. Seen as the home of the *Bibby Stockholm*, it feels a sad and spooky place, a bleaching reef of war's infrastructure. Perhaps that is why the sight of the barge being tugged into the port is so sinister. On a soft summer sea morning this dangerous, diseased, deficient old hulk is dragged out of the twentieth century and into harbour, bringing her promises of mistreatment and misery with her.

She looks as though she might be just about ready to incarcerate anyone, starting with, well… *human rights lawyers.*

The first potential inmate of the *Bibby Stockholm* to come to national attention is an Iranian dissident, arrested in Iran for his work as a human rights lawyer and campaigner, and imprisoned there. Assigning an articulate and impeccable Iranian human rights lawyer to be one of the first aboard is either fate in a dry mood or a laconic and very British piece of sabotage, originating in the Home Office, perhaps, with someone fed up of the brainwaves and brutalities the government requires the department to deliver. Meanwhile, the press do our bit to magnify *Bibby's* fear, simply by reporting the facts. Our article is the first to point out the lack of fire exits, the dodgy water tanks, the rapidly repaired rotten hull, the lack of air-conditioning, the dangerous claustrophobia, and the *Bibby Stockholm's* sinister reputation as a cursed ship.

The cursed ship is made ready. There are protests in Portland against asylum seekers, and counter-protests against the mistreatment of asylum seekers. Placards say *Welcome!* And placards say *Go home!* The coach arrives and the men haul their belongings up the *Bibby's* gangway, even as the Fire Brigades Union condemns the vessel, calling it 'a potential death-trap'. Fifteen men are placed aboard. Another twenty are reprieved after challenges by lawyers working for Care4Calais. Then, on August 7, 39 men are placed aboard. On the same day, tests on the barge's water supply are returned from a lab, showing the presence of Legionella bacteria. All 39 men are withdrawn from the barge and placed back in hotels.

The *Bibby's* pipework requires hyper-chlorination, to flush out the most deadly strain of the bacteria. Palms slap foreheads in the Home Office as the nation comes to terms with our investment in a dilapidated, rotten, disease-ridden fire risk.

The 39 men send a letter to the Home Secretary, begging not to be returned to the vessel, and informing her that one of their number has attempted suicide. The government responds through deputy chairman Lee Anderson.

'If they don't like barges, they should fuck off back to France,' he says. The comments are backed by the Prime Minister.

The pipes are cleaned and the men returned to the barge. Their numbers are steadily raised, from 39 to 300. In October, a 23-year-old from Nigeria, accommodated in an Essex hotel, is told he is due to be transferred to the *Bibby Stockholm*. He attempts to take his own life in the hotel car park – the *Bibby's* first blow. The *Bibby's* first kill soon follows.

On the night of December 11, Leonard Farruku, a 27-year-old from Albania, has a breakdown aboard the barge. Other men hear him shouting, screaming and banging on the walls of his cabin. At some point that night, or in the early morning of December 12, Leonard Farruku hangs himself in the showers. He had apparently told his sister, who lives in Italy, that he was being treated 'like an animal' aboard the barge.

It is not known when Leonard Farruku left his home in

Albania, but it is believed that he crossed the Channel on a small boat the previous August. His death, the press reports, caused 'great distress' to the other men aboard the barge. 'Great distress' would be putting it lightly. Their fear and confusion were exacerbated when the wrong person was declared dead – a Cameroonian man also interned on the barge – leading some aboard to grieve for him.

How many of those people went to bed on the night of December 12 wondering who would be the next to go? The internees report that the food is very bad and in short supply, so that the last of the 300 men queueing for it go hungry. Stepping off the barge onto the quay means being security-searched, airport-style. If you smoke ten cigarettes a day, you get searched ten times.

In a year which has boiled with rhetoric about asylum seekers, small boats, migrants, backlogs, costs, treatment and mistreatment, a Home Office spokesperson makes the following comment on Leonard Farruku's death: 'The welfare of all those in our care is of the utmost importance, and we take our responsibility for their wellbeing incredibly seriously.'

All of Britain, and all the world, if it cares to look, can see that *Bibby Stockholm* is working exactly as she was designed to do. If people are attempting suicide on being told they are being transferred to her, she is working. If being held aboard can drive a brave and resourceful young man like Leonard Farruku, who smiles brightly and sweetly in his pictures, to take his own life, then she is working.

The response of the people of Portland to Leonard Farruku's death appears on a sign on the dock road the next day, along with bunches of flowers:

So very sad
that one of our
friends from a distant
land has died today.
May you rest in peace
Your friends at
Portland Global Friendship

Then, this. Leonard Farruku's family are refused Home Office funding to repatriate his body to Albania. His sister, Jola Duskhu, sets up a GoFundMe page to raise money to bring his body home. In just one day donations reach £18,869. Most are between £5 and £50. Reading the fundraising page swells the heart. It shows a Britain and an Albania of which we hear nothing, suddenly united.

Gillian Fraser
£5
I'm sorry for your loss. Feel ashamed of my country.
He should have been welcomed.

Stephanie Evans
£10
I am so sorry for your loss. I am ashamed of this government
and hope you will not think that they represent the majority of
the citizens of the United Kingdom. My prayers go to the whole
family and I hope that Leonard will be returned
to you as soon as possible.

Ylli Prifti
£20
Sorry for your loss, I paharruar kujtimi i vllait.
['Unforgotten brother's memory.']

John Caldwell
£10
I am so sorry.

Besnik Shabani
£20
Te jem te bashkuar, ngushllime familjes
[To be united, condolences to the family.]

Matthew Styles
£5
I'm so sorry for your family's loss. Please know most decent British people would never want or allow this to happen.

Donna Russell
£5
In memory of your brother. So sorry for your loss x

And on and on the messages and donations go. Leonard Farruku comes here on a small boat. As a young Albanian male, he is among the most demonised of all the groups who cross the Channel. He ends his life in a place which might have been designed to provoke breakdown. He sees and is killed by the worst of Britain. And then, by his death, he shows us the very best.

Calais before the end of summer

Augnst heat leaches into September and Calais is a different town. All along the seafront people stroll and chat. It's an evening to take the children out for crêpes and ice cream, the breeze from the Channel barely cooling the coast. Lovers and friends sit in their cars, looking out over the thick, dark sea, making calls, passing bottles, going and coming again. Later, in the middle of town, halfway down the Rue Félix Cadras, a loose crowd assembles outside La Betterave bar. The bar is almost like any other with its cheerful red facade, outside chairs and tables, its local beers and its jukebox. Yet the majority of the clientele are not white or French. They are mostly young men, and they have a distinctive look – cheap jackets, tracksuits, trainers, and the quick and watchful gaze of the people from the illegal settlements. The gaze flickers at you, asks a question – threat or not? Keeping an eye out when you're in town is the way you live, if you are sleeping in one of the scratch camps in the wastelands, or in the squat in town, or under one of the bridges, or along the railway track.

At La Betterave this evening there are one or two locals, young and boisterous, but the people to whom the bar's welcome speaks most clearly are rough sleepers, refugees and migrants. They drink little but they sit at the tables, lounge in the chairs, use the Wifi, check their phones, gossip, relax and act like people everywhere else. The men have little or no money and the bar is refusing to punish them for it. They are being afforded a space. Outside, I fall into conversation with an artist. He holds himself with poise and he wears a fedora. He must have been about sixteen or so, when he left Eritrea a decade ago.

'I have been travelling for ten years. Ten years! Four years in Germany. And now I am here. In BMX camp, in the Jungle.'

'Where are you going?'

'I am going to Britain. If I can. Somehow.'

'What will you do in Britain?'

'I will go to art school. I will learn and I will teach and I will practise my art.'

'What kind of art do you do?'

In return for a beer he draws a picture for me in my notebook. He takes a long while over it, moving inside, now that he has a drink, taking his place on a stool at the bar and bending over the page with my pen, completely absorbed.

'This is an unusual place in Calais,' I say to the barman.

'Everyone is welcome here,' he returns.

'How do the people of Calais feel about that?'

'I am from here, we are from here, the owner is from here, we are the people of Calais,' he says.

'But in other places these people are not welcome?'

'In other places.'

'So no one minds?'

'My father is a *sauveteur*,' he says: a rescuer. 'Extremely respected in Calais. So I do this and people, whatever they think, they respect it, because they respect him.'

It's not much of a street, Félix Cadras, though it is named after a great Calais man, a lace worker who became a Communist, led the Resistance and was murdered by the Nazis. But it is in the middle of town, the perfect place for an embassy, and it feels as though they have made one here, the owner, the barman, the locals, the musicians who play here and the people who come out of the scrub and the bushes and are welcomed as equals. Between them they have made a little outpost of a world worth fighting for, where people are judged on nothing but their behaviour. A non-racist, non-discriminatory bar should not be worth mentioning, and in its attitudes, its publicity material and social media, La Betterave is mostly about beer and music. But it also campaigns against the evictions of the rough sleepers and publicises the hunger strikes of three Calais residents who came out in sympathy with those they called 'exiled people'. It promotes the work of photographers who document the treatment of the exiled people and the candle-lit vigils held in memory of those who have died on this border.

The artist has finished. He presents his work in my notebook. His picture shows a seated woman, her back to a date palm, one knee up, forearm on her knee, forehead on that arm, either asleep or dejected. She looks like a figure from a Gauguin – I am sure she must be, her hair is the same as his subjects', the same long Tahitian hair tied back – but she is shown turned in on herself, struck with some despair, abandonment, depression. In such a short time the artist has made something striking, vocal. It is only a sketch, barely more than a doodle, but painful and beautiful, and when I look carefully, remarkable. The piece is not made of lines but points, hundreds of little spots. Pointillism without the colours, the dots forming the image of the outline of the woman, the palm's trunk, which is carefully detailed, the dates, exquisitely, and the palm leaves, done in outline. He signs the piece, and gives me his email address, and before I can ask him about the sketch, he is saying goodbye and going back to BMX, the camp in the Jungle.

It's still hot at the seafront. The late ferries are running just offshore and the water is black as cats. The tide is far out. The beach undulates, so you paddle through soft wet sand and then up onto harder ridges where white gulls roost. On flat sand, the water lies in layers as if stacked in moving sheets, first a ripple's edge an inch high, then another on top and more, thicker, a wave a foot high, a rubble of white foam, and another skiing along on top, and you're more than chest deep now. You are deep enough to launch a boat, to put down an engine, to haul someone up over the tube, to push someone off the tube, deep enough to swim or drown.

Along the sand at Blériot Plage, in a couple of weeks, there will be a crush and struggle aboard a dinghy and a 26-year-old Eritrean woman will drown. But not tonight, not on Calais town beach where the sea becomes louder and the rushing wider as you walk into the little ripples, that holiday moment made strange by the night and the huge dark Channel beyond.

You only have to put your toe into the sea to be in contact with water molecules that are in contact with water molecules in a chain that – if you could follow it – connects you to every other molecule and drop of water in the world's one encompassing ocean. I am thinking about this great darkness and about what it would be like to get into a flimsy dinghy now, in a rush of adrenaline and scrabbling hands. Dover and Calais both occupy outcrops of coast. These are not sheltered ports. It took huge breakwaters, moles and piers to make harbours of them. This is not a sea for second chances. This corner of the world-ocean is a wrench of currents, compressed and flooding tides. You cannot quite see Dover tonight but it is just over there, in that glow that will become a prickle of lights as you leave this shore behind.

The artist comes down to the liquid black one night. He has been waiting for the call for weeks and it has come, and now the tide is far out and he is with a large group, including several women and children. The boat is pumped up in the dunes around midnight. A dozen men lift it onto their shoulders and carry it down to the beach. Out, the smuggler says, take it out, and he wades along with them, fixing the engine to the back. He tells the artist to bring the petrol tank, and the artist struggles into the water with it clutched across his chest, thick plastic, reeking of fuel. The tank is heavy but he wishes it were heavier. Is there enough inside? He wishes he knew about engines, about fuel. One of the men brings a stack of plastic bowls that the smuggler has handed him, and as soon as the boat is floating lumpily in the waves, the water starts to come in over the fat tube and the smuggler shouts at them: Get in, use the bowls, get the water out.

He does not have to say, *Pray the British pick you up. Pray for the British, pray the British will come.*

How much fuel do we have? the artist shouts. You have enough fuel to go all the way, the smuggler says, and then they are into the boat and the engine is running and they are going into the liquid black. They are cold and soaked through from the wading and they are all praying.

The artist stares at the blackness, at the lights of ships, at the fear. Calm, calm he tells himself, calm, they all tell themselves, do not admit the fear, do not admit the hope, do not admit the possibilities of anything but – so far so good, so far so good, so far. They keep coming. The helmsman is barely out of his teens but he keeps the tiller and the throttle steady. He may be a steady soul or he may be frozen with fear, but either way he keeps them bearing into the black. They pray they do not break down and drown. They pray the tube does not deflate. They pray the engine does not stop in French waters, or all this will be for nothing.

Prayers are not much against the size of the sea. But the engine does not stop. They do not know anything about the currents or the tide, the tide which was so far out when they launched and is starting to turn, starting to haul an inconceivable weight of

Atlantic seawater from the south-west towards the north-east, up-Channel, slowing them only a little at first, and pushing them off course to the north. The boy keeps them bearing on. One hour, two. It will not be morning soon. Ships and lights in the darkness, and Britain ahead. They can see them clearly now, the lights of the tall transiting towers on the cliffs of Britain ahead. They all shiver, packed together. Parents give the children water. The artist watches the sea, willing it to stay calm, praying it will stay calm, the weather forecast is good, the sea is supposed to stay calm, but far out here it heaves and rolls like a beast in half-sleep.

The artist does not know it, but if he falls into the sea, after hours cramped on a boat like this, his legs will not work. The RNLI have seen it often: a few seconds in the Dover Strait's typical temperature of seven degrees or so will wind him, hammer his heart and gasp his breath. He will hang helpless in his life jacket, which may or may not work properly. He will not have the strength to haul himself into a rescue boat, should one appear. Just a few moments in this sea will render him utterly helpless.

There is a shower of rain and the wind is stronger but the prayers are working. The tube is not going down, the engine is running and what water comes into the boat – every slap-splosh of it a terror – they bail out with the bowls. Six hours and a grey paling behind them, over France. The day, the light, will come. And, though they do not know it yet, the British will come. Dover lifeboat will come.

Imagine the artist is brought ashore. Imagine he survives internment in a barracks with his mind and spirit intact. Many people do, after all. His claim is granted – 93 per cent of Eritrean asylum claims are granted – and he gains leave to remain in Britain. He survives being kicked out of his accommodation and turned loose. Some kind of fortune, connection, family, stroke of luck and extraordinary resourcefulness (it takes all of them, a glittering alignment of the stars) sees him make a life in Britain. He meets someone and he falls for her and she for him, and they have children.

One day in Britain, early in the twenty-second century, one of the artist's grandchildren finds themselves talking to someone, a conversation which drifts to histories and heritages. Suddenly both of them realise they have a grandparent who took a small boat from France.

Really, yours too?

Where did he come from?

He was from Eritrea. He was an artist! And yours?

She came from Sudan, she carried my mother, two years old…

How proud you would be, if you were one of them, or there with them, witnessing their meeting. Not just proud of the people who crossed but proud of everyone who helped them, in any way, over the whole long impossible journey. The twenty-second century will come, our descendents will live here, and like us, they will all be from somewhere else. The largest-ever study, a twenty-year project conducted by the Wellcome Trust Centre for Human Genetics at the University of Oxford, found a typical white British person living in England shares 40 per cent of their DNA with the French, 30 per cent with the Germans, 11 per cent with the Danes and 9 per cent with the Belgians. Apart from the Welsh, whose DNA is the closest to that of the hunter-gatherers who came to Britain after the last Ice Age, walking across a flooding Doggerland as the glaciers melted and the waters rose, we *all* came by sea (or air, or Channel Tunnel).

★

The next morning I cross to the other side, to Dover at the end of summer. England is wearing her dog-days green, the hedges bursting, the brambles heavy, the port flooded with holiday traffic returning from the Continent. I go down to Tug Haven and the Lord Warden. Processing has shifted down the quay and is now called Western Jet Foil. There are higher fences and more complete barriers, so you can see nothing but the car park, the tents, and, when they emerge, the coaches that transport the people from processing to holding centres. People have been crossing successfully enough to bring two agency photographers down, looking for a picture.

One is talking to another on his phone. They're thinking about tracking one of the unmarked coaches that carry the people away into England. I ask him about it. 'You can follow the coaches a certain way, but then you tend to lose them and it's not worth it. A lot of them just go to London,' he says.

He talks about Napier, the barracks in Folkestone which has become notorious. 'There's one point where you can see over the fence through the long lens and into the rooms. It looks bad. Hot and horrible. You really wouldn't want to be in there.'

I ask if they have seen the Newsman, whom I first met here.

'Yeah, he's around. Still doing his thing,' one of them says, and grimaces.

It is hot today. I go down to the beach where men have spaced themselves out at intervals along the shore, fishing. I flop into the water and float in the yellow-green sea. The power of it is absolute. You hang in the shallows, a fleck on Dover beach.

9

Calais in storms

Come winter, Gess is back in Calais, with her own charity, Gessica Helps Refugees. It consists of little more than a donations page on Peoples Fundraising, in which she states her case:

> My name is Gessica and I have been volunteering with refugees in Calais for nearly four years. I work with many of the fantastic charities here, but the help I provide to refugees is niche. As an independent volunteer, I am able to spend all my time in the field with the people who live here, getting to know them, listening to their stories, sometimes just letting them talk. They often tell me this emotional support is what they value the most. To do this work I need your help...

Gessica's main source of publicity is Clare Moseley. In October Clare writes describing Gess and her work:

'It will soon be getting very cold in Calais, particularly at night, and so many people are sleeping outside with no shelter. It is grim beyond words and all help is vital. Gessica's living expenses are minimal as she lives in a caravan and spends little on food, but she has run out of money...'

In November, storms Ciaran and Babet come. Clare is in Calais again, taking donations to Gessica. Even years of work with the rough sleepers have only partly prepared her for what she finds. This time, she says, it is horrifying.

The tent line at Old Lidl is now shrunk and huddled, the shelters with their bright-blue tarpaulins teeter on flooded paths and patches of ground which have turned to ponds. All around the tents are mud-coloured pools strewn with refuse, plastic bottles, bags, trash and broken things. Wooden pallets have been pulled up to the entrances of the tents. You can imagine wobbling and tip-toeing between them, soaked anyway, and the rain still coming down. Clare finds young men with torn cagoules, boys in flip-flops with wet socks, boys in flip-flops with no socks.

'It broke my heart to see people living like that,' she says. 'There are many people without proper coats or shoes, and this November is much colder and wetter than normal. Seeing young boys living outside without even the basics to keep warm and dry is devastating. When you shake their hands, they feel like ice.'

Then Clare adds, 'The ray of light was the generous donations from you, my fabulous friends, that enabled Gessica and I to buy warm waterproof coats and sleeping bags for those who were most desperate, and give waterproof boots to a few of those we met who had literally no shoes and were in flip-flops. There are many more in need, but for those we could help, the difference it made was immeasurable.'

In December, Clare writes again:

> Last week something amazing happened. Thirty brand-new tents were delivered to my friend Gessica in Calais because of wonderful people who care about others in need. It has been so incredibly cold in Calais recently, especially at night, and this stock will mean Gess has emergency supplies for those who are most desperate: late-night arrivals; tents that collapse in the night in high winds; people who have no one else to ask.

★

In January I call Clare. She is on her way to Calais, driving another load of donations.

'How is Gess?'

'Ah, she's had a really hard time because her van broke down. We raised the money to buy her a van but then it broke down. And the problem is that the mechanics in Calais aren't very good and a lot of them don't like the refugees. But we got donations to fix the van and it's hard to go back to people and say we need *more* money because the van broke down again.'

You read Clare's appeals, and picture the struggle Gess is engaged in, and imagine the stress she is under. And then you see or hear the news and people are in the same conditions as the rough sleepers in Calais, only they are in Gaza and being bombed, too, and they are in Ukraine and missiles are falling on them, and one of my friends in London writes to me and says, 'It is a horrible time to be reading the news. I have to not think about it very much, as I can't help and don't want to live in it.'

I have to not think about it very much, as I can't help and don't want to live in it.

We have to stay sane, after all, and do our work and live our lives and love and support and give joy and hope to those we love and those who need us, and so *I have to not think about it very much…* Thousands, tens of thousands, are quite reasonably thinking like this; an editor I work with at the BBC says: 'News avoidance. We're seeing it more and more. People are just turning away, because it's so awful.'

★

But think of Gess and Clare, and the thousands, the tens of thousands across Britain and Europe like them, who run towards the fire, to help. And often they – you – we - are the same people; we hide from despair when we cannot stand it, and we run towards it, to fight it, when we can.

Over 12 million people in England, over a quarter of the population, volunteer to help others at least once a month. Rates have fallen from the all-time record set during the pandemic, when a magnificent third of us helped others. But a very large section of the British population are still determined to help, and within that group, a number are drawn to help refugees. Clare gives me contacts for one of them, Cosima Doerfel Hill, known as Cosi, on the Wirral.

I am looking for the last pieces of this story: what happens at the end of the road, when people who come through Calais and cross the sea are processed and enter our asylum system. I want to know who they are, what they dreamed of, what they found and what is happening to them. I want to know who helps them, because those people and this place are also us. So, tell me about the country you found here. What is this place? What are we really like?

10

Britain in winter

The cold has come. After months of storms and rain we have forgotten winter's bite, the smell of clenched ground, the dusty chill. Across the flat lands from Manchester to Liverpool, the trees are stippled twigs against a monumental sky which is wearing two coats – duffle-grey low down, fumbling white higher up. The clouds lie in ranks like dim keels, a hundred ships drawn up over the plain. I am going to meet young men from the Kurdish regions of Iran. In photographs, their homeland is mountainous, with flushes of green meadows under rock slopes and huge escarpments, sand-brown in summer, snowed in winter, bright under pale-blue skies.

Here, the back gardens of Newton-le-Willows have been abandoned to winter. A lone figure walks a white dog across a field while two herring gulls watch, fat as sheep. On the train, a woman tells her phone that she is going to sue another woman over an eviction… *People always underestimate me, I'm gonna make mincemeat of 'er…*

For New Brighton, you change at Liverpool Lime Street to the metro. Merseyrail's trains are bright-yellow and filthy, toys left out in the mud, but they are on time. In the underground, a boy with a swing in his step gives an elderly busker a pound. Liverpool James Street has a ghost platform, apparently left over from the 1960s. The train sets off to the ting ting of a tram bell.

This is the England the people from the small boats have

come to: *The next station is Hamilton Square, please change here for trains to Ellesmere Port, Chester and the U-boat story*, runs the display board at the end of the carriage. R S Thomas once accused Wales of 'worrying the carcase of an old song'. The people I am going to see came ashore under the Dover spitfire experience and have made it as far as the U-boat story. No offence to the glorious dead, but we really need new songs, too.

Two travellers gossip and laugh when one thinks she has missed her stop. She still has Africa in her accent, his stubble is grey and their smiles are identical as they laugh ruefully about mishaps. We emerge at Birkenhead Park. High gorse bushes by the track are in flower, a tiny riddling of summer gold. 'I stop here,' says the lady, and she wishes the stubbled man a good day.

In New Brighton the sea is as flat as a floor and stone-grey but it is good to see it. The tall cranes across the Mersey have their booms up, not working. A sea priest told me that they had to strengthen the defences around the Port of Liverpool because there were cases of migrants and refugees, disillusioned by what they found in Britain, attempting to stow away to Canada. There is a gay defiance about Victoria Road's strip of cafés, food shops, florists and hairdressers. Our meeting place is bright-blue, pink and leopard-print, its name in rock 'n' roll lights: *Rockpoint Records*. This café-bar with its worn-in feeling of a thousand gigs is another embassy, like La Betterave in Calais – Rockpoint hosted a bake sale to raise money for asylum seekers who were accommodated at the Grove House Hotel on Merseyside.

Cosi Doerfel Hill is well known here. She comes through the door like a gust. 'Hello hello! Thank you so much for travelling all this way!' she cries, as though she is inconveniencing me, rather than being taken away from her work at the Citizens Advice Liverpool. There is a touch of Scouse and another touch of richly precise second-language English in her speech. Her face is crinkled with smile lines. Cosi's background includes study of maritime trade in the Hellenistic Period; the Octopus Project, which she founded, providing educational experiences and play days for children; the In Limbo project, supporting Europeans after Brexit; and, professionally, coordinating access to advice and justice on behalf of Citizens Advice Liverpool. Cosi speaks quickly.

'In February–March we had these protests against asylum seekers in Knowsley and then again a month later half a mile from my house, at the Grove House Hotel. What could we do? We had no idea. I'm a migrant myself and I feel I need to be alert to how other migrants are treated. I started asking, *What do they need, the people in the hotel?*'

The protests in Knowsley, outside the Suites Hotel, were as violent as any Britain had then seen since the small boats began arriving from Calais. A police van was set on fire. Stones, broken paving slabs and fireworks were thrown at riot-armoured officers. Three were injured. Fifteen people were convicted of violent disorder.

The faces of the convicted give a sense of who can be mobilised to scream hatred at people they have never met, and the police protecting them. Men with grey faces in their forties look as though they are in their late sixties. Men who could tell you exactly what happens to the poor and left-behind of Merseyside, to men and women and boys who find their passions stoked to rage by the bubbles in their phones, who itch for action, for anything beyond the every-shabby-day, in left-behind districts of left-behind towns, where thousands wait for housing, for jobs, for help that does not come.

'My neighbour thought we should make the refugees cakes,' Cosi continues. 'I thought that's very sweet, but what do they actually need? They were all single men at the Grove House – they get the least sympathy in the official narrative, "fighting-age males", the lowest of the low. But the manager of the hotel was *lovely*. He said there had been trouble but the police came and it died down. He said, "What they actually need is boots, not food. We can't accept food because elsewhere in the country it has been spiked."'

'You're kidding.'

'I know. Some people really are that vile. I got involved on social media and I got death threats, threats to me and my children, and I had to get the police involved. But I linked up with local people who were helping, including a lot of trade unionists.

'Every Friday, the Patriotic Alliance were coming to protest at the hotel – it turned out to be exactly the same people as at the protests in Knowsley. There is someone we know who is on all their networks who lets us know what they are doing – they are in their Telegram groups and they're an expert on the links between the different fascist networks.

'So every Friday we turned up, too, in bigger numbers, and within four weeks their numbers dwindled to zero. So now we know – if you get an infestation of fascists, turn up! They moved on to that hotel in Wales, the same people.

'What they had done was spread allegations about assaults on people in the area, and asylum seekers bothering local school girls. It was all lies – people who live locally already *knew* the asylum seekers, they'd been playing football with them in the park, they knew they were good lads. But there were other people who got the wrong narrative, so I thought, *more community building* – as migrants ourselves, we need to be in solidarity with these people!

'I am from Germany, and the narrative creates a pecking

order – as if German or French immigrants are more acceptable than Polish people, and asylum seekers are at the bottom. So as someone with relative privilege, I must fight for them. If I don't, there will be nobody to fight for me when I get attacked.'

Cosi's fight looks like delight, like giving, like joy. Her fight includes organising a meal in a restaurant for Eid, providing football boots, organising bake sales, taking 'the lads' to football games in parks and to local festivals. She's helped organise dances where Kurds and Ethiopians could perform and teach. She was involved in the planting of a memorial tree to people who drowned in the Mediterranean. She describes a 'Global Liverpool' event she helps organise, a collaboration of many community groups:

'Fifteen asylum seekers volunteered as helpers. They were thrilled to be able to contribute something rather than always having to accept charity. They loved sharing their culture. We had many compliments for how kind, welcoming, friendly and helpful they were. This is a part of Liverpool where xenophobic narratives are rife because the locals are struggling with severe poverty and migrants are often blamed. This group of asylum seekers did a lot in that one day to change people's hearts and minds.'

I ask her about what has happened at the Grove House Hotel since she became involved.

'Most of the lads were dispersed from the hotel at the end of September. There is a cluster of them in Ellesmere Port, in a house. They get next to nothing. In the hotel they got meals, and £9 a week. A bus ticket is £2 one way, a day pass is £4.60, so if you're on £9, even if you don't buy soap or sanitary products or toothpaste, you can't afford to go out for the day more than once a week. Now they get £45 a week asylum-support, and that has to pay for food, clothes and bills.'

'What is the situation with their claims? Have they been granted asylum?'

Cosi snorts. 'Some of their claims haven't even been submitted. They have been given questionnaires to fill in: *How were you tortured? If you have no documents, could someone in your home country get your documents to you?*

'It is only available in English, so you have to get it translated. The people in Ellesmere Port are only 20, 21, they're boys – just boys. Obviously you need to try to get a lawyer. Legal aid only pays for very few hours' work, so unless it's an open-and-shut case, firms don't want to take it on because the money is so low. The going rate for taking on a claim is about £1,200.'

'Did you know,' she says, 'they're not allowed to access English as Second Language classes until they have been here *six months*? How ridiculous is that? And they're not allowed to work, and they can't do voluntary work but they can volunteer, so they have to be careful what wording is used if they want to volunteer somewhere, to make sure it will not get misinterpreted by the Home Office as "voluntary work". Not all charities are aware of the difference, so many cannot take asylum seekers as volunteers. Ten per cent of the volunteers at Citizens Advice Liverpool are refugees. And people think they get phones and SIM cards from government support. They don't – if they have mobiles and SIMs, they're from charities. Which reminds me, I've got to send two phones to families in a hotel in Wallasey today. I put out an appeal and a woman sent me £70 for a phone.'

'You know,' she says, '40,000 people coming in a year – it's not even half a football stadium! People crossing the Channel in 2023 was 4 per cent of immigration, 4 per cent! You must tell this story – we are all migrants. We are a migratory species. Migration is a human right.'

★

Here in Rockpoint Records, Cosi is wrapping her arms around friends, talking at great speed, promising to send something and receiving promises that she will be sent something, and then baklava appears on our table, and almond biscuits, and Cosi is greeting another friend, and everybody knows her and now she is hugging Mo who has come in with Jag.

Mo is broad and stooped, wearing a woolly hat and an uncertain expression until he greets you with a huge smile. Jag wears a smart suit. There is the precision about his appearance and manner of a young man going about a business-like life. He comes from Yemen, and claimed asylum here having lost his job in Dubai, he explains. Jag now works for a law firm as an immigration adviser.

Cosi and Jag talk rapidly. Mo is carrying a small red apple and a jar of cloves. Carefully, painstakingly, Mo is pushing the cloves into the apple, side by side, covering the whole surface. His English is limited but he shows me a piece about the Kurdish tradition of the clove apple on his phone. The clove apple symbolises love and communication, so a girl might present one to someone she loves, or a mother might give one to a son as a peace offering after an argument. They are powerful ancient symbols and this one smells as sweet as an Eastern spring.

I ask Mo about his journey here: why Britain?

'Because my father said Britain is best. My father paid for me to come. He said Britain is best.'

'What does your father do?'

'Farmer!' says Mo with his great smile.

'Sheep?' I ask, 'My mother farms sheep!'

'Apples! Apple… what is the word?'

'Orchard?'

'Apple orchard!' he nods. 'Yes. Orchard.'

'Why did you leave Iran?'

'I am Kurdish. I make protest. Here I show you…'

On his phone is a form with his statement requesting asylum.

It says he went to a protest against the government, and afterwards the police came to his house looking for him.

'Will that get him asylum?' I ask Jag.

'If he can provide evidence,' Jag says. 'If he can provide photographs of himself at the demonstration, if he can provide evidence then yes. It is hard – they want evidence of political persecution from friends or family, but getting that evidence can be dangerous. Political asylum is much harder than religious asylum now. If you can prove that you are a Christian and that you went to church, then you can get asylum, but they will interview you and if there is any discrepancy, they will reject your claim. It's case by case. The Third Country Unit check the route they have taken, then serve a letter – you have 14 days to justify why you are claiming in the UK. If you have not been registered in a third country – Greece or Italy or wherever you entered Europe – you are likely to get limited leave to remain. That's not a visa or asylum.'

'And what happens to someone who gets limited leave to remain?' I ask.

'Mostly they just wait,' Jag says. 'And most of them are waiting for solicitors, but most of the solicitors are closing for asylum cases – legal aid is £419. It doesn't cover the work. We charge £1,000 for everything. For most of them, for that, we can get the claim settled. We take a full witness statement of five or six pages, life history from childhood, and we go all the way from there.'

The difference between the two young men is dizzying. '*You* didn't come here on a boat!' Cosi teases Jag. Jag laughs. He has means, education, connections and drive behind him. He is working, helping people, paying taxes, supporting his young family here. Mo has his apple, which he continues to spike with cloves, and his phone, which he looks at, distractedly. When we speak of asylum seekers or when we speak of refugees I know, at least in theory, we are talking of whole spans of humanity. But not until you sit with these two at the same table do you really see it. They have nothing in common, except the need to leave home and their longing to build their lives here.

'Who do you deal with most?' I ask Jag.

'Most people are Kurds, Syrians, Iranians, Sudanese. They all get a positive decision – because of war and politics there are very high rates of clearance for these people and these countries.'

'And what happens to them when they are cleared?'

'Then they make a Universal Credit claim. Their weekly payments stop. Then they get an eviction letter, from Serco etcetera, and then of course they approach the council. But the council cannot always help them.'

'And what will happen?' I ask. 'What will happen to all these people?'

Jag becomes very animated, even by his lively standards.

'There is a gap between these people and integrating, because most of these people are illiterate as far as the UK job market is concerned – they are not able to find work. What is needed are refugee employability courses – start training them to be compatible with the market! And there are cultural issues. You might find an Arab woman saying, "How can I work as a cleaner?" And then if you have five kids, you can't go and do a night shift.'

'So what do we need to do?'

We are standing now, away from the table, talking intensely.

'If the country designs a programme to close the language and employability barriers, *this* will make the difference! Otherwise they can only do delivery jobs and this is *not* helping society. And then it's easy for them to be drawn into bad stuff, lots of opportunity for selling weed. And a lot are not self-motivated. I know ONE guy, he came from Sudan, he self-educated himself in English, he got himself to the Government IT bootcamp – and now he has a Masters in computer science and he has a job. Others prefer to work in delivery because it's easy, cash in hand, they can avoid tax. The government doesn't ask you to work in return for citizenship. In Germany you have to work. But here you can wait five years, do casual work hand to mouth, and get UK citizenship.'

'That seems crazy!'

'*This* is the barrier! If you can train these people, then they can work and they and their children can make a contribution. Their children will, because they will go to schools and universities and get jobs, but these people? I don't know.'

And we look at Mo, who all this time has been pushing cloves into his apple, unable to follow what is being said. Now Jag has to go, and we shake hands and touch our hearts, and another man joins us, bringing the story I have half-longed and half-dreaded to hear.

11

Luton is beautiful

It is dark outside now. In Rockpoint Records the red and blue and yellow lights form atmospheric pools on the tables, the album covers and posters. *A dream you dream alone is only a dream. A dream you dream together is reality*, drawls John Lennon.

Jiwani is tall and angular, dressed in black. His hair is neatly cut, his eyes dark and mobile above high cheekbones. By his fluent English and the way he carries himself, he could be a mature student. He is in his early thirties, I reckon, though it seems rude to ask. He sits next to Cosi, opposite Mo, who sits next to me. On the table between the four of us are bowls with the remains of the baklava and the almond biscuits, and a carton of mince pies which the lady behind the bar donates, unasked.

'Where are you from?' I ask Jiwani.

'Iran,' he says, 'I am Kurdish from Iran.'

'When did you leave?'

'The first time was 12 years ago. I took a truck because of my family. If you don't do military service in Iran, you can have no job, no money, no driving licence, no passport. I put military service off and began smuggling between Iraq and Iran, taking things from Iraq that are banned in Iran, like alcohol. Then I was injured in an explosion – something left over from the Iran–Iraq war. I couldn't go to a public hospital. Nine years ago, ISIS took over Iraq and many people left for Germany – they let everyone come. I followed them to Germany because it was a year and my injury was not healed. They treated my hand and said, "You will never get any kind of help if you don't apply for asylum. You need to give us a reason to give you asylum."

'I wasn't a refugee. I was there only for hospital, so they said, "We're deporting you." But if you get deported back to Iran it's bad, they accuse you of snitching on the regime. So I went back – France – Turkey – Iraq – Iran. Then after a few months I started smuggling again, this time passing messages from the Kurdish party in exile in Iraq into Iran. They caught us giving out messages in the villages. I escaped. Turkey. Two weeks. You know, Turkey uses refugees to push the buttons on Europe – we're Erdogan's red card on Europe. If you don't do what Erdogan wants, he can open the gates to Europe. The KDPI [the Kurdish opposition to the Iranian regime, in exile in Iraq] paid for me to take a truck. I went. I looked out of the truck in a European country I don't even know. The language, the script was Russian, Cyrillic.'

'Sounds like Bulgaria,' Cosi puts in. 'There is a crossing from Turkey into Bulgaria.' She listens intently to Jiwani as he speaks, her chin resting on her hand.

'In April last year I arrived in the Jungle in Dunkerque. We were a group of 50 or 60 people then. I just followed orders from the smugglers. If you don't do what they tell you, they say, "You have paid for this, we are just finishing our job." In this democratic country, France, I saw the smugglers firing pistols in the middle of the night. I saw them fighting, making themselves bloody. The first time they wanted us to cross was a foggy day – you couldn't even see five metres. It was very very cold. I jumped out of the boat, I said, "I'm not going anywhere!" I said, "I'll stay in France." And this is when they said, "You have been paid for. We are doing our job."'

The Migration Observatory in Oxford, the British institution engaged in the most painstaking and sophisticated studies of the Channel small boat crossings, reported on this phenomenon in a briefing, 'People Crossing the Channel in Small Boats', which concludes:

'In some cases, research also suggests that the decision to come to the UK is influenced more by smugglers, agents or handlers than by the migrants themselves.'

An entirely different life-story awaits him in France. But the smuggler has this plan, this destiny for Jiwani.

'I lost my shoes and my clothes – they don't let you take a bag. The second time, three hours before the boat was ready, the smuggler pushed me into the water – three hours being really wet and cold. I had to walk from Calais to Gravelines, wet and cold, to the bus and back to the Jungle. With no shoes. Four or five hours.'

Jiwani looks aggrieved as he tells this – like a man giving a bad review of a travel company. Presumably Jiwani could have walked away from the Jungle, from the smugglers. But where would he go? What would he do? Who can judge Jiwani? Those who have not found themselves in the hands of a violent gang on the edge of France with the vague promise of some sort of better life ahead of you, and only the wastes of Calais and Dunkerque all around?

I noticed this plaintive note in Calais, this helplessness, along with a kind of peevishness, when some of the rough sleepers approached the charity volunteers. Living on handouts seemed to reduce some of these brave, resourceful people to a kind of juvenile dependence. I recognise it in me. I know that tendency in adversity to lay your anger and discomfort on someone close to you, perhaps on someone who is trying to help. As I listen to him, I am picturing myself in Jiwani's story. There I am, trudging sodden and cold along a grim road, for four of five hours, slogging back, defeated, to an illegal slum. I can see and hear myself in his place, my spirits sinking into a resentful bitterness, soaked and indignant, pissed off with the whole thing.

This is half of our reaction to the small boats – there but for the grace of God go all of us. *We'd do the same, wouldn't we?* as people in Dover put it. We feel distress and anger and impotence, empathetic projections of us as them. Perhaps it is the urge to push these feelings away that makes us prey to the other impulse, the one that sees an 'invasion' of 'migrants'. When we are scared, anger is a more comfortable reaction than impotence or despair.

It is the might with which the battle against despair and impotence is fought by people like Cosi, Clare Moseley, Gess, Kay Marsh in Dover, by the RNLI, by the charity volunteers, by the kind security guards in the rain and by the man we will meet in a moment, which gives them such light and force. They cannot see it, perhaps, from inside their own lives, but to the observer it is unmissable.

By doing what they can, they are energised, filled with purpose and meaningful action. They may be haunted and angry at the desperation and scale of the task of helping, and assailed by terrible sadness, as Gess and Clare say they feel often, but somehow their souls and spirits are enlarged by the help they give. You can see it in them as clearly as you can see them. Looking at them, you feel their hearts have been made great. You would wish that feeling on everyone. You would wish it on entire nations.

Jiwani's story continues. He was part of several failed attempts to cross the Channel.

'This happened five times – once the boat was stolen, once the police came, once the boat was not ready, once the boat was sunk by old sea defences. When they wanted to go, they pushed us to jump aboard. You haven't slept. You're afraid of the French drones, the French police, so you go in the middle of the night. The last time we saw another boat going, they said "You're next", and they got us to pump the boat up.

'I don't know how to describe the crazy, angry sea. It was very scary. The first 500 metres are very scary – the boat was like a carton on the water.'

Jiwani picks up the box of mince pies and undulates it up and down, a boat in surf. He puts it down and drums his fingers on it.

'With 50 people, the water comes in with each person who gets into the boat – 10 to 15 centimetres of water in the boat, and you are sitting in it. This Vietnamese woman behind me was pushing so hard on my back.'

Jiwani mimes being pressed forward from the waist, his head bent down to the table, wincing, 'And I said please, stop pushing, but she couldn't – there was no room.

'We left at 9 o'clock at night. In the middle of the water, who hears you? An Afghan guy pointed a laser pen at a French drone so they knew where we were. A French ship follows us but it can't come close because they are making waves. They used a big light, a laser, to point us to the French shore. Our driver was an African man and he was very good because he didn't listen to anyone!'

'How did you find your way?' I ask. 'The map on your phone?'

'No, at sea you lose signal. The smuggler gave the driver a compass. He said if you keep the needle between that number and that number you will be fine, otherwise you could go anywhere. This driver was very good. Because he drives, he did not have to pay. Sixty people shouting go this way! Go that way! And he didn't listen! I think it was five hours on the sea.

'Then the English coastguards came. Ten minutes before, I was thinking how many metres down to the bottom of the sea.

You are so scared, which we call ghosts in the mind – every wave comes, splashes in, your death is five centimetres away. When the English coastguard came it was like an angel had come down to us. No one can make it without the English coastguard. The boats don't have enough fuel or enough power. In five hours you go so slowly. We saw the UK flag on the boat. It was a very happy moment for us. I forgot my wet clothes. I looked at the sky and I thought – I have done it.'

Jiwani puts his head back and looks at the ceiling of the café and closes his eyes. 'I have done it.'

We all watch him, head back, eyes closed. Now he looks at us and smiles.

'And they took you to Dover?' I ask, after a moment.

'Yes. At Dover I was very tired, sleepless. It was a long time but they were *right* to check us, to check our fingerprints, to check we were not smugglers, not criminals. I had a very, very strong hunger. They gave us some sausage. It was delicious!'

His face breaks into a great grin and we all laugh with him.

'I wanted more sausage but they said there were too many people – that day I think twenty boats crossed. They changed our clothes, gave us dry clothes and shoes. I thanked them from my heart. They took our wet clothes and put them in a plastic bag and locked it. They gave us some crisps and a small drink. They took our fingerprints and sent us on a coach to a hotel not far away. Sheer something? I saw the sign through the window.

'They called my name and said you will have an interview. I was very tired. Not slept in the Jungle, crossed on the boat, not slept. I said, "Can I have an interpreter?" They said, "No, your English is good enough." I said, "Can I postpone it?" They said, "Yes, but then it will be up to you to arrange," so I said, "OK. I do it now." This is why my name is spelled wrong on the forms.

'The next day they took us to Luton. For the first time I saw what England looks like. At each step you have a goal in mind. Is this the safe place I have imagined? Luton is a beautiful city!

I saw two or three neighbourhoods. The hotel was near the airport – it was a beautiful place. You can never get a better place. It was perfect.'

Jiwani is smiling and shaking his head at the memories of the hotel and Luton. We are all smiling back and I am grinning at his pleasure and the thought of Luton's beauty, asserted with such delighted conviction. I ask, gently, 'How long were you there?'

'I was there for a day and a half. Then I was moved to Wallasey, to the Grove House Hotel. And I was there for five months.'

'What was that like?'

'The Grove House was great! A cool place, cool friends.'

He grins at Mo who smiles back and nods emphatically. They both laugh. Cosi sees the query in my expression and says, 'He missed the protests. By the time he arrived, it was fine.'

By overwhelming the far right with support for the asylum seekers, Cosi and her fellow counter-protesters had made the area safe and welcoming again.

'And then where?' I ask Jiwani.

'Then I was moved to Ellesmere Port. It's a small city. I have a very small, square space, a box from there to there. I don't have anything.'

He does not look upset or aggrieved. This is not voiced as a complaint so much as a statement of fact, though the space he indicates, between the TV on the wall and some shelving, is barely two metres.

'And what do you want to do here?' I ask.

Jiwani's face changes. He is filled suddenly with clarity and vociferous determination.

'What do I want to do here? I want to be a voice for my people. I want to be the *sound* of my oppressed people. I went to London for marches against Iran. I have not been granted asylum yet but this – this safe place? This *is* asylum.'

★

As I am writing this down we sit for a moment in quiet, the music playing. A barman who has just started his shift throws a packet of crisps to a friend in the window.

And then Jiwani says: 'It is easy to tell you, but you can't imagine waking up in the Jungle and waiting for a charity organisation to help you. Each time you go for the boat you lose everything – the smuggler makes you throw away everything. You lose your tent, your sleeping bag, even your coat because it is too big to wear under a life jacket. The smugglers make you leave your bag in one place, and then if the boat doesn't go they take you back another way, so they can steal from your bag. The Jungle is a crazy place. Once I came out of the water and got back to the Jungle, there was some sun and I was drying my clothes and some Dutch Christians came to religionise.'

Jiwani tells a detailed story of debating theology with the Dutch proselytisers in his underpants. He re-enacts challenging them over possible interpretations of Deuteronomy, chapter 18, verse 18, as we all laugh. I can see he is on the point of setting about proving the point to me again (that the coming of the Prophet Mohammed, according to some Muslim scholars, is predicted in the Bible) and I head him off, and I ask:

'And what do you think of Britain?'

'Britain?' he says. His expression opens and he looks at me very frankly. 'Britain is good for us, bad for you. I don't mean foreign people are bad for you. And I don't mean to make a criticism, but there are too many old houses. The quality of life is under... it is low. Look across the street, you see that white open building? Have buildings like that! Not all these *old red walls*! Especially in Ellesmere Port, these old red walls are sometimes driving me crazy. Let the cities be more beautiful. I don't complain. They saved my life. They've given me asylum. *This* is asylum.'

What did you expect?

The first people I spoke to about the small boats crossing the Channel turned the story I thought I knew upside down: the security guards who go to stand in the Dover rain, in their retirement, in order to help make people welcome, to be part of a Britain that makes them proud. And I saw the silent, dazed people in the coaches, and I imagined that the terror and stress of the crossing, and seeking asylum does that to you: silences you, cows you, drops your head. But not necessarily. Not for long. Not for Jiwani, who stepped off the rescue vessel and walked up that ramp into Britain, a political dissident, a refugee whose ambition is not to take shelter and merge into the background, but to stand up for his people and his beliefs and fight for freedom in Iran.

I feel different impulses as I listen to him. The KDPI has been in revolt against Iran since 1945. Kurdish groups have been fighting for space and self-determination since at least the ninth century. In our era, there seems no chance that Iran or Turkey will ever give up land or sovereignty to the Kurds. Only absolute and unlikely changes of the regimes in both those countries could possibly bring Kurds land or political freedom. Jiwani's cause is surely as lost as it is just.

Hopeless, I think, looking at him across the table – *this is mighty and this is hopeless*. And, of course, no one has any right to tell him this, or anything like it, and shame on me for thinking it, for what freedom was ever won without the belief that it could be? And what a compliment Jiwani and people like him pay to Britain, in their certainty and their experience that this is a place where a just fight can be waged in safety, with the sympathy of the populace and the solidarity of his exiled people.

While we fly Spitfires over the White Cliffs and tell the U-boat story, we should remember, too, that harbouring political dissidents and governments in exile defined us in the past and still defines us now. We did not ask the opponents and victims of Hitler or Stalin or Putin what they could contribute to our economy; we welcomed them because we believed then, and we still believe now, in freedom and in justice. That should be enough. The regime in Tehran is abominable, and Jiwani is here to fight it. But still I ask him what he does for a living and he says, 'I am a graphic designer. I can design sports clothes on a computer – I can do everything except sew them!'

And I think *Do we need graphic designers?* and look it up later. Indeed we do: the UK is short of them, according to the Home Office's Shortage Occupation List. It is a £3.6 billion market which is expected to grow over the next five years. Britain needs Jiwani – and I think I understand why he needs Britain, but still I press him:

'Why come to Britain? Why not stay in Germany? Britain is worse for housing, for quality of life, diet, education and health than France or Germany – why not go there? You even speak good German!'

Jiwani agrees about the housing. In Germany, he says, they do housing inspections, and much that is acceptable in Ellesmere Port would fail. But the difference is political freedom, personal freedom. He says it several times: 'Freedom is the most important thing!'

'I am not criticising Germany,' he says. 'The police are right to control, to check, because Britain is harder to come to, but drugs and criminals can come up easily through the Balkans to Germany.'

As he says this, Jiwani looks at me anxiously. It had not occurred to me that people we designate 'migrants', 'refugees' and 'asylum seekers' should be as perturbed and fearful as we are at the thought of criminals and dealers arriving from overseas. But of course they are. Living more marginal and insecure lives than the settled population, they have even more reason to be distressed by the thought of dealers, gangsters and crooks. It is ironic that the newspapers, the bias-bubbles, the frightened, the bigots, the racists and the hard-right media should raise such froth and fury over the figure of the criminal asylum seeker, while asylum seekers themselves are drawn here partly by their impression and their experience of British policing, law and order.

Jiwani explains that the conflict between Kurds and Erdogan's Turkey spills over into Germany. He lists Kurdish activists and political figures killed by Turkish and Iranian agents in Europe. The murders go back decades.

I understand, I think, but I push him again, 'But why Britain?'

'Because in Germany you are not *safe* like this. Not *free* like this.'

And he tells a story of a Turkish woman filming him at a Kurdish demonstration in Germany. She told him there was no such thing as Kurdistan, no such thing as Kurdish land. She frightened him. 'Was she a spy?' he asks. This would not happen in Britain, he believes, because in Britain there is freedom, he keeps saying.

'Because this is where I am *free*. This is where I am safe.'

It is wonderful to hear it, this echo from Calais, this echo from across the world. It is a huge and heartfelt global compliment, to a country that seems to struggle to feel proud of itself. And I look at Jiwani and think that although Britain would surely love to see an Iran in which people are free to drink alcohol and the Kurdish population is respected, a man who smuggled booze and dissident literature into that country might not be the first person you would put on a poster celebrating official British values – although as far as actual British values go, Jiwani is surely in many of our hearts.

The official values that we teach our children and that schools have a duty actively to promote are democracy, the rule of law, individual liberty, and mutual respect and tolerance of those with different faiths and beliefs. Jiwani stands for all these things. The UK has placed sanctions on the same organisation that hunted him for his promotion of the Kurds – the Iranian Revolutionary Guards. All our values support him. Democracy, law, liberty, respect and tolerance are our core beliefs, in as much as the state is able to define them, and Jiwani's belief in Britain, and what he has found here, are a confirmation of them.

According to the evidence of Jiwani's experiences, and his feelings about being here, this is what Britain *is*. And this is what his story proves, and what the stories of the thousands who have come here and who wish to come here prove. Britain is actually as good as Britain is believed to be.

Now Jiwani shows me a letter from the Home Office on his phone. The letter confirms that he has passed the third country check, and that his claim for asylum will now be processed.

'He was so scared when he got this!' Cosi cries. 'Look at the language!'

The language and phrasing are archaic, ponderous and framed in plodding negatives, as if this is a letter from a depressed institution that struggles to see any positives, and so it takes a moment to see that this is good news. The substance is that you have been checked and have cleared this stage. You have moved to the next stage, and here is a telephone number you can call to check the progress of your claim.

'Cosi,' I say, 'Isn't that actually rather good? They're working on his claim, and there's a number for him to call.'

'You can call it, but this is never answered,' she says.

'But – hasn't Britain actually done well? Pulled him out of the Channel, fed him, given him dry clothes, hotels, food, money, now this – isn't that good?'

Cosi looks surprised. 'But the system is so full of flaws and mistakes, it could be a thousand times better.'

'Sure, but – as far as what Britain has done so far... shouldn't we be rather proud? Haven't we done better than most of the world's countries would do?'

Again, Cosi looks surprised and doubtful. So much of her astonishing energy is devoted to helping people stuck in the system, and in miserable places, in themselves and within it, that the idea that the system might be praiseworthy is wrong-footing. 'I would say that the system needs very, very many improvements,' she says, finally.

No one would disagree. This turns out to be the one assumption I held at the start of this story that I will still hold at the end. But the fascinating part of the system, it keeps turning out, are the individuals within it, who defy every preconception and assumption. One of those individuals is Neil.

Front Line Man

Neil does not exactly bounce into Rockpoint Records, but he is light on his feet and deft in his gestures; he has a kind handshake and eyes that see you softly, somehow, but really see you. Being regarded with quick curiosity and withheld judgement makes you feel strangely open. Within moments of meeting, I find myself conversing with him in unguarded frankness. He makes a reference to his age and I yelp.

'You're never! But how on earth do you look so young?'

'Honestly? I think it's the giving?' he says, and his laugh at himself and his sincerity is so disarming we both laugh. 'You know you give and you get back?'

This is a strange inner-Britain front line, where the people who crossed the Channel in boats sit around a table beaming at one of the people working for the outsourcing giants – one of the men and women who run the so-called 'asylum-seeker hotels'. I do not know quite who I was expecting when Cosi said she would introduce me to a Serco manager, but it was definitely not Neil.

Serco's profits are in the hundreds of millions, its shareholder payouts in the tens of millions. Asylum-seeking is making it fortunes upon fortunes: a £1.9 billion contract to run hotels and accommodation in 2019 has become a titanic golden goose. In the year to March 2024, the Home Office spent £3.1

billion on hotels alone – Serco (£250 million profit for asylum in 2023), Mears (£50 million profit from asylum in 2023) and Clearsprings (£90 million profit from asylum to Jan 2024) take the lion's share of the £5.5 million *daily* hotel bill in 2025. A Serco manager made me think of a tough-faced man in a suit. Neil is neither. He ran the Grove House Hotel. Serco wants to promote him, but Neil wants to stay on the ground, working with people.

'How did you get into this?' I ask.

'I've been working with refugees since back in the *day*,' he says, and grins. 'I was taking people off trucks in Dover when there was *nothing*, nowhere for them to go. I'm one of the founders of Migrant Help. You had to do everything – there was nowhere for them to go, no clothes, no food. I had a 23-year-old girl in Dover who was injured, there was no bed. I found her a space in an old people's home. The woman there said, "Bring her!" An old people's home...' he says, and shakes his head at the memory.

'How do you do it?'

'Well, I don't manage hotels. I manage people – I look after them, help them out, keep in touch with them. Had one guy from Trinidad. I said "What are you doing? We don't have refugees from Trinidad!" He said, "The police want to shoot me, and there's a gang after me." His grandmother got him a ticket to Britain. Every night I spoke to her on FaceTime, telling her he was alright.' He laughs at this, too. 'Every night!' He could be talking about a wayward grandson.

Like all of the men who were accommodated in Grove House, the Trinidadian has been moved on, dispersed into accommodation.

'What's it like after they leave the hotels?' I ask.

Neil nods. 'For the most part the housing is OK. They're local authority homes so they have to meet a certain threshold. But they're all the ones that are hard to let, the ones in *areas of concern*. A lot of the lads are getting thrown out of hotels and being sent to areas where they suffer hostility from the local people. So I go down and mediate with the locals, explain who these people are.'

I picture angry people in tough places with indignant voices and legitimate, insoluble grievances – 15,000 people are waiting for affordable homes across Liverpool. Placing asylum seekers in the poorest communities, which is routine because it's cheaper, guarantees hostility.

'*Mediate*? How does one do that?'

'It's not always easy. There's been some shouting! But I knock on the door, show some ID, say, "Have you got five minutes?" and explain to them what's being done. They'll often give me exaggerated stories of behaviour that they've seen online or heard – there can be a bit of shouting. But I ask them to tell me exactly what they have *seen* done, and I'll invite them to come with me, to walk through my hotel, and I'll pick someone at random and introduce them. The lads are mostly quite well educated – the poor can't afford the fees, you know? They may not have qualifications but most of the lads have been to good schools, good for where they come from. And because they get to meet each other, that changes it.'

'What's it like for the lads, being in hotels?'

'In Germany, they can work – but they can't work here. So they feel undervalued. They're not giving back like they'd like to. They really want to give back. They offer to clean and cook, they want to do anything useful, but we have to explain that they can't. So I'll come in and find they've washed my car, or dug the flowerbeds. In the case of the Grove, the owners were most sympathetic. Since the hotel was closed and everyone dispersed, they've still got six or seven people every day turning up asking for food or clothes, and the owner won't ever say no to them.'

Neil glances away, and then down, and then back to me.

'The women and children are the really hard ones,' he says.

His voice changes slightly, quietens. 'The kids can't go outside, you know. It's really upsetting. People are crying, it's really hard, really emotional. They're being moved from the Holiday Inn in Hoylake, and getting moved into houses. But they're trying to put two families into one house. That's hard work – when there's two sets of kids. I want to open Grove House back up.'

'Open it back up?' I repeat, astonished. 'But that would fly in the face of everything the government is doing.'

'Yeah, I know. But that would be 80 spaces for overspill! *80!*

14

Front Line Woman

In Calais it is a brutal stormy winter. One day, Gessica's donations page disappears. I message Clare – is Gess OK?

'Yes, Gess is ok but it is not going to work out her working without the support of a big organisation. It's a shame, but it is what it is. Calais is horrific right now, too.'

I am alarmed to hear it, imagining the strain Gess must have been under and her feelings at having to stop the donations page and halt her work. So much of this story seems to demand to be filmed, to be made into a defiant and beautiful drama – indomitable people in dire circumstances, striving for better lives and ways to help their families; extraordinary men and women defying everything in a mighty struggle to help them. But this story does not end in a clear victory. It leads to hundreds of thousands of small and difficult and unfinished victories. Its heroines and heroes are everywhere.

Clare grows up on Merseyside and becomes a chartered accountant, then a manager for Ernst and Young, then a senior manager at Deloitte. She is a committed volunteer for the Prince's Trust, giving 15 years' service providing free tax advice for start-up businesses, and receiving two awards for outstanding volunteering from Prince Charles.

Then, one morning in August 2015, she finds herself reading

about refugees in Calais, horrified as much by the readers' reactions as she is by the article.

'My heart sank as I read the comments,' she later writes. 'There was so much cruelty. These people whose suffering was so much greater than anything I had experienced were being dehumanised, talked about as though they were rats. It made me feel sick. I thought: I don't want to be like this. I want to show that there are people in Britain who care.'

And so she fills her car with donated clothes and drives to Calais. She first volunteers for a French charity, L'Auberge des Migrants, but very soon she starts Care4Calais, which becomes the most effective link between the rough sleepers and anyone in Britain who wishes to help.

Her battles are unrelenting, she later tells an interviewer for *The Connexion*, beginning with the expectations of the volunteers who come to Calais to join her.

'There were lots of volunteers turning up. But what they wanted to do was find five or six refugees, make friends with them, find them everything they needed, and get a really good feeling from it. But that means 30 volunteers are only helping around 200 people. With a system in place, those same volunteers can help 6,000 people. Volunteers don't really want to load 400 sleeping bags in a van and come back later and put 400 jumpers into a van and go out again and put 400 pairs of jeans into a van. So I had to be quite strict with them and say, "You've got to think about what we're trying to achieve." It wasn't always popular. It was difficult, but it was very, very necessary.'

Clare is an unmissable figure in the wastelands, tall and pale with fair hair, which makes her distinctive from a distance. In Calais, I watch her constantly answering questions, directing and redirecting volunteers, breaking off to speak with lawyers, the police, the press and the authorities in France and Britain. She is oblivious to the wind and rain whipping around, her gaze in constant motion, checking the distributions, the work of the volunteers, the needs of the rough sleepers, the demands from her phone. She is simultaneously a political leader, general, sergeant and soldier.

Clare learns law, publicity and social media, fundraising, logistics, aid, distribution and handling the press all at once, as they arise. She is named 'One of Six Women who made 2015' by *The Guardian*, alongside Charlotte Church.

In 2016, the camp known as the Jungle is demolished. Over 6,000 people lose their shelters, which ranged from tents to shipping containers. Clare estimates there were 9,000 people in the Jungle at its height. Over 3,000 become rough sleepers on Europe's north-west coast, with large numbers around Calais and Dunkerque. When the police begin to enforce the 'no fixed points' policy, destroying tents and shelters, these people now depend wholly on charities, principally Care4Calais, Secours Catholique and Auberge des Migrants. In 2017 Natacha Bouchart, Mayor of Calais, signs a decree banning the distribution of food from fixed points. Care4Calais will eventually overturn this.

In 2018 interviewer Vicki Broadbent asks her to describe her ambitions. Clare replies: 'To develop Care4Calais so that, as a charity, it can help more refugees across Europe, not just in Northern France. We are hoping to go to the Italian border early this year, and maybe even Serbia. I would also love to find more time for campaigning. It's desperately important that more pressure is brought to bear on the UK government to play a greater part in the refugee crisis. I know there are so many people in the UK who want us to be doing more. We are a strong country, and we should be able to do more in what is the biggest humanitarian crisis of our generation.'

In January 2019 she gives evidence to the House of Commons Home Affairs Committee on English Channel Migrant Crossings, chaired by then Shadow Home Secretary Yvette

Cooper. Clare is asked why the people she is helping wish to come to the UK. The first two reasons, she says, are family and language, and then:

> The third reason that we hear, which is, I hope
> something that you will be very proud of, is that a lot
> of people, particularly from Africa, say that they really
> believe in the UK as being a bastion of human rights
> and democracy and things that they don't have in their
> countries. They believe that these really high ideals are
> the things that they want to have that they don't have.
> Some of it even dates back to colonial times. You hear
> this from people from Sudan especially. They say that
> they have grown up learning about how the UK is the
> place that has all these ideals that they want to aim for.
> They believe in safety, freedom and democracy and that
> they will see that in the UK, which I think is amazing.

The fact of Clare making this point, there in front of a parliamentary committee, entering it into the record of the country, making it precise – this vision of Britain as Britain wished to be perceived seems to have taken particular hold in Sudan – and inviting the MPs, Yvette Cooper especially, to share a national pride in the standing of Britain abroad, matters. This is why they come, and we should be proud to know it.

As the numbers crossing the Channel in small boats tower upwards, drawing people to and through Calais and Dunkerque, the pressures on Care4Calais and Clare increase from every side. In August, a 16-year-old Sudanese boy is found dead on the beach, killed by hypothermia. With a friend, he had broken into a shed, stolen an inflatable and two shovels they intended to use for oars, and set out to cross the sea. The dinghy capsized. The boy could not swim. Care4Calais volunteers stand in silent memorial for him. At the same time, in England, the Charity Commission opens an inquiry into the management and governance of Clare's organisation.

Now she is fighting on all fronts. Since starting Care4Calais, donations totalling more than £340,000 have passed through her personal bank account. Clare points out that this decision saves Care4Calais £3,000 a year in foreign exchange fees. The inquiry accepts that none of the money was misused or misappropriated. But the organisation is now turning over £2 million a year and after three years, during which the inquiry lays a constant demand of stress and time upon her, the Commission concludes that, coupled with 'poor minute-taking' and 'conflicts of interest which may have existed', the arrangement was 'inappropriate' and had put the funds 'at risk', which, it says, amounts to 'serious misconduct and/or mismanagement'.

It seems a lame conclusion after such a raking search. Nothing went wrong, but it might have done, so you're guilty.

The effects on Clare are visible in the photographs taken around this time. She is thinner, her eyes tired – but there she is, standing outside the Home Office addressing a 'Refugees Welcome Here' protest she organises in tandem with Stand Up to Racism, demanding the government recognise the rights of undocumented refugees. Her face has lost some of the light and certainty you can see in the woman who first arrives in Calais, but none of the resolve.

While Clare deals with the Charity Commission, and fights actions in the courts on behalf of refugees in France and England, thousands of people are still arriving in the wastelands and heading for the sea, and every day Clare's volunteers do what they can to clothe them, feed them, provide shelter and lift their morale, intervening howsoever they can. The pressure tells on the volunteers and on Clare. During an argument about photographers taking pictures of the rough sleepers, Clare loses her temper with a volunteer. The volunteer makes a formal complaint and Clare apologises for inappropriate behaviour 'in the heat of the moment'.

At an aid distribution in Belgium, Clare uses pepper spray in self-defence. Witnesses to the incident confirm that she was threatened, and no complaint is raised against her, but it turns out that while pepper spray for self-defence is legal in France, it is against Belgian law. Clare apologises again, and continues to carry the spray in France.

Now lawyers for Care4Calais, working to Clare's direction, challenge the British government's Rwanda deportation plans, taking their case to the High Court, and at the last minute, to the European Court of Human Rights. The ECHR court rules the first Rwanda flight illegal, grounding the plane just 90 minutes before it is due to depart. This ringing victory for Clare and the charity draws fury from across the British right and the government, including Boris Johnson, who accuses their lawyers of 'effectively abetting the work of criminal gangs'.

Clare has been accusing the government of the same thing for years. By refusing to provide safe and legal routes, Great Britain keeps the people smugglers in business, she argues. And when in 2023 Clare steps down from Care4Calais, leaving the charity she created in the hands of a new CEO, Steve Smith, the soon-to-be-sacked-again Home Secretary, Suella Braverman, pays Clare the compliment of a personal attack. Responding to the Charity Commission's findings, Braverman says:

> It's clear that some charities and civil society groups are actively undermining efforts to curb illegal migration. They form part of an establishment committed to ever-increasing migration, with no regard for the will of the British people. These groups are comprised of politically motivated activists masquerading as humanitarians. It is a con. But the British public won't be fooled.

(Well, not the vanishingly small section of the British public who suffer from Braverman's levels of misanthropy, anyway.)

Towards the end of November 2023, the Supreme Court delivers a unanimous verdict on the government's Rwanda deportation scheme: it is unlawful. The government then resolves to make a law declaring it lawful, which seems to sum up something dingy and disillusioned in Britain's soul that winter. But in the aftermath of the judgement, I speak with Clare, and although she knows Rwanda will return, she is joyful.

'It was such a big moment! To hear that judgement, so clearly and so strongly – for everyone to hear that judgement was so important. I was really losing hope, but then such a clear judgement, given like that!' she exults.

Lord Robert Reed hands down the court's findings with painstaking clarity. He cuts a modest figure, as if he might have been overpowered by a judge's wig and scarlet robes, but the Supreme Court does not, on this occasion, go in for regalia. He speaks with a precise and soft voice, his dark tie a funereal touch, giving every word its weight as he carefully buries the government's case: Rwanda is not safe, for there is no guarantee people sent there will not be returned to places where they are in danger. Watching him, you have a sense of an old and deep-set form of British power speaking, something more measured, more intelligent and more certain than the bluster we are accustomed to hearing from politicians. This actually is Britain, you might think, observing the scene. Thoughtful, rigorous Britain.

'*That* is who we are,' Clare says. 'That is a country I can believe in.'

★

In the spring, the doomed Conservative government responds to the judgement with the comical Safety of Rwanda (Asylum and Immigration) Act 2024, which declares the country safe, and anyone transported there also safe from ill-treatment or refoulement. The Houses of Commons and Lords stall and amend the Bill until it is passed, pointlessly, in April, in another colossal waste of time, energy and public money.

Clare returns to her family home in Merseyside. If she feels bitter that she should have left Care4Calais under criticism from the Charity Commission for what might have gone wrong, and to the jeers of her defeated enemies, whose plans for Rwanda she helped to undo, she does not show it. The decade of effort and life she gave to her fight has left her scarred and exhausted, and proud of what she was able to do – especially proud, she says, of stopping the deportation flights. I ask her if there was any story from Calais she remembers most strongly, anything to stand for all those battles and all that care.

'My mind is too full of them,' she says. 'There is nowhere to begin.'

The way we tell it

Bibby Stockholm and Rwanda were never solutions to the problem of the small boats crossing the Channel, or anything else. They were ludicrous, cruel, wasteful absurdities, symbols of a refusal to think in any decent or sensible way about how nations should deal with refugees, or how human beings should deal with human beings, or with change, or with reality. The Rwanda scheme cost £715 million, and resulted in four failed asylum seekers volunteering to be flown there. Four.

The boat and the scheme are cancelled by the incoming Labour government in July 2024. Instead, this government goes after the smugglers with new energy and more money. The smugglers respond by cramming more people into even less seaworthy boats, according to the Refugee Council. All the smuggler has to do, a penetrating report by the Global Initiative Against Transnational Organised Crime points out, is place a boat in the water anywhere along 250 kilometres of coast. The territory is divided between different gangs, overwhelmingly Iraqi Kurds, who compete but also cooperate in load-sharing and sending out surges of dinghies. Cellular structures mean there is no controlling mafia which could be broken; the 'mafia' referred to in the scratch camps of Calais and Grande-Synthe are enforcers hired by the gangs to extort money from the rough sleepers, to charge them for access to aid provided free by NGOs, to terrorise and exploit those who have not purchased 'package deals' from the smugglers.

A just-in-time route to market sees would-be travellers held well away from Calais and Dunkerque until the weather apps look favourable, whereupon trains, taxis and even chartered coaches bring the people to the coast. Towards the end of 2024, as British and European governments and their law-enforcement agencies prepare their biggest, most coordinated and best-funded raids against the gangs, the smugglers mount the busiest December day of crossings on record. Nine boats take 609 people to sea; they are all rescued and landed safely in Dover.

As the Global Initiative concludes, in the industrialised process of smuggling people across the Channel, breaking an individual gang has yet to defeat the problem, or even significantly dent it: 'The higher the obstacle, the more people will turn to smugglers, who, in turn, will charge more for riskier approaches to infiltrate their clients into the UK,' it reports. The first successes under the new government also reveal the towering scale of the task. In France, 18 Iraqi Kurdish smugglers are jailed in November 2024, 100 boats and 1,000 life jackets are seized. Just this one trial, involving police forces across Europe, generates *67 tonnes* of paperwork. The ringleader was already in jail, convicted of attempted murder. He had been controlling the operation from his cell.

Meanwhile, over 36,816 people made the crossing in 2024, the second-highest total, at the cost of 78 known deaths recorded by the French authorities. However, the United Nations' Missing Migrants Project marks 82 deaths, including 14 children, making 2024 the most deadly year so far. Crossings in the first three months of 2025 are the highest ever. Enforcement is not stopping the boats. 'Smash the Gangs', like 'Stop the boats' is meaningless. What to do?

★

The most widespread idea, and the most adamantly called-for, is the provision of safe and legal routes allowing refugees to apply for asylum before they risk their lives in the Channel. Safe and legal routes are demanded by the UNHCR, the Red Cross, humanitarian groups, NGOs, agencies specialising in the study of crime, and every think-tank which takes a balanced view of the problem. The Public and Commercial Services Union, which represents members of Border Force and Home Office staff, also calls for safe and legal routes. Few institutions have seen more of this issue than these two, which are charged with the delivery of government policy.

Enforcement *can* work, it has been demonstrated in the United States, if it is run alongside the provision of safe and legal routes. The Refugee Council's January 2025 report, *Deaths in the Channel – what needs to change*, cites the success of introducing safe routes to the US alongside border enforcement: the combination reduced monthly attempts to cross the Mexican border from 200,000 in 2022 to 54,000 in 2024.

In early 2025, the American president's withdrawal of any route to asylum, his cancellation of refugee resettlement (excluding white Afrikaaners from South Africa), threatened mass deportations and the shrouding of the American machinery of governance in a miasma of fear and chaos choked flows across the border to a trickle. There is no indication of any appetite for such policies in this country, where between 63 and 72 per cent of Britons report 'unfavourable' views of the President of the United States, according to IPSOS. Talking and listening to Britons suggests that a reasonable interpretation of 'unfavourable' is a combination of fear, loathing, incredulity and disgust.

Where safe routes have been tried by Britain, they have worked. Syrian refugees were eligible for a resettlement scheme until 2020. Very few tried to cross the Channel in boats. Since the scheme ended, Syrians have consistently been among the top nationalities in the dinghies, according to the House of

Commons Library research briefing in October 2024. The briefing points out that a similar scheme for Afghans failed to prevent many taking to the boats, because the scheme was too small and too difficult to access.

Opening visa processing centres in the biggest asylum-claiming countries and on the Continent would allow the approved to come in safety. This worked with Ukrainian refugees, who were able to apply for visas at centres in Europe, provide biometric information, pass checks, and come safely to the United Kingdom. Since most Afghans, most Eritreans and most Iranians, for example, are granted asylum, nationals of these countries could be cleared in the same ways. This would erase chunks of the backlog, save time and money, and moreover, empty the boats.

A wide spectrum of British people are in favour of safe and legal routes. A survey for the British Futures think-tank conducted by IPSOS in July 2024 found that 50 per cent of the British public support the idea of a humanitarian visa which would allow up to 40,000 people a year with strong asylum claims to be resettled in this country. Unfortunately, the government currently rejects the idea of opening safe and legal routes, dismissing safe routes as an unfavourable alternative to enforcement, though the US experience shows this is a false opposition. The announcement of a humanitarian visa, ministers must fear, would be a gift to the far right, GB News and the Reform party. Here again, our politicians seem less confident, less imaginative and less humane than the people they represent. We stand ready to help. We want to save people from the gangs and the sea. Are we are too frightened to be ourselves?

As a society, IPSOS polling found in 2024 that we confuse immigration and asylum. On average, we believe that over one third of immigrants are asylum seekers. Two thirds of Reform voters believe that more than half of all immigrants are seeking asylum. The actual figure is 7 per cent. Populism thrives by distorting the national understanding: IPSOS found the Reform party is both most vocal on the issue, of all parties, and the least representative of average public opinion.

And so our very British silence, a compound of unease and confusion over asylum and the small boats, risks ushering the hard right to power. The journalist Gaby Hinsliff interviewed young men at a Reform rally, an event she described as, 'Three hours of speakers attacking small boat crossings, "woke" ideology and grooming gangs.'

'I'm a great history lover,' a Reform-supporting 16-year-old boy in a blazer and spectacles tells her. 'I can look back over the past – the great voices in the Second World War – and see a Great Britain. Today when I look around, I don't.'

A 24-year-old explains that Reform is 'the only party standing up for British values.'

'The young men I meet in Leicester seem less angry than nostalgic for a past they're too young to remember,' Hinsliff comments. She concludes: 'Above all, they're desperate for something to feel good about.'

Could a country for which people the world over risk their lives, and which saves those lives in their tens of thousands, be seen as something to feel good about? What would happen if we captioned the pictures of people coming ashore in Dover as enduring British victories in a global competition for labour, talent and commitment?

Refusing to contemplate meaningful change in how we view and treat the small boats crossings catches every government in the same trap: as far as the British are concerned, cruelty still has its limits. Although Home Secretaries have shown themselves capable of prolonged, attritional cruelty – in Calais,

in the detention centres, in the entire 'hostile environment' –
the country is just not prepared to allow them to go far enough.
Hitherto, governments have committed to deterrence, but for
deterrence alone to succeed, it has to be intolerably cruel. Sir
Keir Starmer has praised the 'remarkable progress' made by one
of the leading proponents of intolerable cruelty, Prime Minister
Giorgia Meloni of Italy, whose policies have dramatically
reduced central Mediterranean crossings.

The success of Meloni's strategy rests on paying the Tunisian
and Libyan authorities to inflict violence, intimidation and
outright horror on refugees and migrants, and increasing
their chances of drowning at sea. InfoMigrants, a reporting
body backed by broadcasters in France and Germany and an
Italian news agency, identifies multiple incidents of Tunisian
authorities deporting people to the desert borders of Libya and
Algeria and abandoning them there. InfoMigrants documents
deliberate attacks by the Tunisian authorities. On the night of
November 7, 2024, a boat carrying 80 people went down off
Sfax, the main departure point for people trying to reach Sicily.
At least 52 are believed to have drowned. According to multiple
sources vouched for by Majdi Karbai, a Tunisian opposition
MP, the boat was deliberately and repeatedly rammed by the
Tunisian coastguard, which denies the allegation. Italy has
supplied the Tunisian and Libyan coastguards with powerful
boats intended to prevent crossings. How exactly they go about
this task is in the hands of their operators.

The Libyan force is notorious for its use of beatings and
gunfire to herd people ashore and into the country's network
of detention camps, dominated by criminal gangs, where
mass murder, systematic torture, rape, organ 'harvesting' and
human trafficking are routine, according to the UN, Amnesty
International and multiple news organisations. Over 20,000
people were raked from the coast and the water and fed into these
camps in 2024. This was a great success for Meloni. Numbers

making it to Italy across the sea fell by 60 per cent from 2023, and the British Prime Minister visited her to learn lessons.

You wonder whether Starmer admires the means Meloni pays the Tunisians and Libyans to employ, or the other prong of her strategy which targets rescue vessels, forcing them to make long voyages to distant ports after each recovery, and there tying them up in legal challenges, depriving the Mediterranean of search and rescue. One of the biggest charities, Médecins Sans Frontières, withdrew its ship *Geo Barents* in 2024, citing the impossibility of carrying on under Italian law. *Geo Barents* had saved 12,675 people in 190 operations. Violence on the beaches, attacks at sea, dumping people in the desert, abusing them in torture camps and the dismantling of search and rescue are the substance of Meloni's 'remarkable progress'.

No doubt Britain could cut Channel crossings by 60 per cent and more, should our flirtation with these policies become a full embrace. We would need to fund and encourage the French police to attack people on the beaches and ram their boats in the water, which has begun. A joint investigation by *The Observer, Lighthouse Reports, Le Monde* and *Der Spiegel* revealed powerful French police vessels destabilising dinghies setting out from Calais, driving them back. The investigation found that officers now use pepper spray on people in the boats, and have begun entering the water to slash dinghies with knives. France is planning changes in the law to allow the authorities to intercept boats offshore. So-called 'beach pushbacks' are a response to the smugglers' 'taxi boat' system, whereby large inflatables are launched quickly with one or two people aboard and driven into position in the surf. Passengers then wade out to them. These are frantic developments, but they are insufficient to dramatically reduce the crossings.

Actually stopping the boats, based on the Meloni model, would mean lining 170 miles of the Channel coast, from De Panne in Belgium to Dieppe in France, with pushback vessels and police. It would mean withdrawing the Border Force boats, stopping the Coastguard search and rescue operations, and banning the RNLI. Britain has never behaved this way. As a nation we are most charitable, in order, to children, cancer sufferers, animals, birds and lifeboat crews. If their appeal cannot defend us from the compassionless abyss, nothing will. The country would be appalled by the cruelty it would require to make deterrence alone actually work.

An astonishingly brave wave of industry, energy and hope has arrived in Britain, where labour shortages and an ageing population create a great need for it. What would happen if Britain were to accept the life and labour these people are offering? Would public opinion – and what is reported and framed as public opinion – permit a change of course, a change of seeing?

You might never guess it from reading our papers or watching our screens, but Britain is in favour of making asylum-seeking work. The National Centre for Social Research's 'British Social Attitudes' survey found clear majorities in favour of allowing asylum seekers to join the labour market. 'Between 2013 and 2024', the survey found, 'support for asylum seekers being allowed to work increased by 5 percentage points among Conservative supporters (from 46 per cent to 51 per cent), compared with an increase of 29 per cent among Labour supporters (from 50 per cent to 79 per cent).'

We are clearly changing with the times, and ever more willing to look again, even at our biggest decisions. In 2024, 57 per cent of Britons polled regretted leaving the European Union. The change of head and heart is particularly striking among Leave voters. As the country enters the second half of the 2020s, the National Centre for Social Research found a steadily growing proportion of the public favour another referendum on Europe – the demand currently stands at 51 per cent across the public as a whole, and when 'don't knows' are excluded, rejoiners outnumber leavers by 57 per cent to 43 per cent.

In the spring of 2025, chaos across the Atlantic and the apparent collapse of the 'special relationship' has helped to turn the majority of Britons towards Europe. Polling by the Policy Institute at King's College London finds 53 per cent are for allying with Europe, 31 per cent for America. This matters in the context of the small boats because there is no possibility of another referendum on EU membership in the next five years or the foreseeable future. British politicians, and the professionally outraged sect of the media which influences many of them, are out of step with British people.

The result is a compassionate, idealistic country, struggling to recognise itself in the way it is portrayed and led. Neither the populists, the far right, the online bubbles, the migrant-bating press, nor the mobs that combination mobilised in anti-immigrant and anti-Muslim riots in the summer of 2024, are anything like the truth of us. The truth of us is a fortunate country, on the threshold of vast change. The United Nations High Commission for Refugees forecasts that at least a billion people will be displaced by climate change in the next 45 years.

'Climate niches,' the science writer Gaia Vince points out, 'the range of conditions at which species can normally exist around the world, are moving polewards at a pace of 1.15m (3.8ft) per day.'

Vince argues that inevitable and unstoppable migration will mean a rethinking of borders, the role of the nation state and how we see ourselves, as our species moves polewards. The good news is, migration does not necessarily make us poorer: in fact the reverse is true, she points out.

'What if we thought of the planet as a global commonwealth of humanity, in which people were free to move wherever they wanted? Today just over 3 per cent of the global population are international migrants,' Vince writes. 'However, migrants contribute around 10 per cent of global GDP or $6.7 trillion (£5.9 trillion) – some $3 trillion (£2.6 trillion) more than they would have produced in their origin countries. Some economists, such as Michael Clemens at the Center for Global Development in the US, calculate that enabling free movement could double global GDP. In addition, we would see an increase in cultural diversity, which studies show improves innovation.'

As the wise and far-sighted Vince knows, merely describing the reality of climate migration provokes hostility and denial: pointing out that opening borders and mass movement will be solutions to it is a minority position, at best. But the heatwaves, floods, fires, cyclones, droughts, famines, snow-bombs and storms to come will not be stopped by denial. Nor will the refugees fleeing them. As the rate of this monumental change increases, more people will cross the Mediterranean, and more will come to the coast at Calais, and more will take to the Channel, and more will arrive on the Kent coast. If we are to have any hope of managing today, tomorrow and the future which is avalanching towards us, we must see and exploit the goodness and potential in this story. The alternative is the story we have been living with, which ends with mass-internment of desperate people and the squandering of all they offer by a shame-faced country, too cowed to do anything the future requires, tangled in deliberately distorted visions of a U-boat and Spitfire past that would be embarrassed by us.

This story, as it has been told to and by the nation, misrepresents everyone. Brave and resourceful people crossing the Channel in hope and belief have been disfigured into faceless threats. The volunteers, organisers, aid workers and very many members of the public who help and support refugees, migrants and asylum seekers are slandered, denigrated or ignored. The populace of Britain, who are as overwhelmingly kind, sympathetic and generous as the people in the small boats believe us to be, are made to feel fearful, mean and foolish. All the good we and our institutions have done has been redacted.

And yet, almost invisibly, almost unreported, our tangled response to the small boats crossing the Channel also flowers with the quiet and mighty goodness of the best of us, and our forebears. The people in the death-trap dinghies bet their lives that this country is compassionate, kind and free. In placing themselves in our hands, they also inspire and find that compassion, kindness and freedom in us. The Britain they believe in is the best country that we are, and the best we can be.

Afterword

The people and institutions of this story, representing so much hope and good and giving, are owed all our thanks, and, for their time and trouble, especially mine.

Cosi Doerfel Hill is working on eVisas for Citizens Advice (which will allow people to prove their immigration status), and preparing to apply for funds for the next Global Liverpool, 'Celebrating the roots and routes which brought us to Liverpool, this wonderfully welcoming city of refuge!'

Kay Marsh continues to work for the Samphire charity in Dover, giving frequent interviews to the media about irregular migration and what we should do about it: granting safe and legal routes.

The RNLI celebrated its 200th year in 2024, over which time it has saved over 146,000 lives. Along with HM Coastguard and Border Force, it helped to ensure the safety of over 36,816 people in the Channel in its bicentenary year. The Dover RNLI lifeboat station has moved to a modern building at the end of a new quay. The new station displays no plaques of historic or recent rescues for passersby. The RNLI went to the aid of small boats in the Channel 114 times in 2024, saving 1,371 people.

Neil returned to his work, managing people from all sides of the debate on asylum.

Jiwani has been granted refugee status. He is now able to work in the UK, in any profession and at any level.

Jag continues his work as an immigration adviser.

Mo was refused refugee status and is facing deportation. He has made an appeal. In the meantime, he is a regular blood donor to the NHS and has found a voluntary role giving haircuts to homeless people.

Gessica Lastrucci left Calais, intending to work on rescue vessels in the Mediterranean.

Clare Moseley has stepped back from her extraordinary decade of fighting for the people of the wastelands and the backlogs.
'I don't regret it. I would do it again,' she says, 'But that's enough now.' Of the current government's policy she says, 'Smashing the gangs won't work, it has never worked, it's just rhetoric. Starmer has to say it or the world would fall on his head. You could stop the boats in two weeks by providing safe and legal routes across the Channel.'
    Of the wider issue, she says, 'You could keep giving £3 billion to outsourcing firms and hotel chains, or you could clear the backlog and give £3 billion to Blackpool Council, and all the other councils where they need people and money. They'd do a much better, much cheaper job of housing and integrating people.'

The small boats are continuing to cross the Channel. Smugglers are responding to increased enforcement by using larger craft, risking the lives of up to 100 people at a time.

Calais recently saw the largest demonstration of solidarity and support for refugees, migrants and exiles, and the largest protest against deaths at sea and on the border, for years. One icy winter day, over 600 people gathered and marched through town commemorating the dead, demanding an end to the suffering and the dying, and calling for safe and legal routes.

Dover's front line has changed. As the spring came in across the sea, I went back to the Lord Warden and what was Tug Haven. There were acres of sand and boulders there, attended by bulldozers and tipper trucks, but no water. The inner docks have gone. Tug Haven has gone. Even the channel to it has gone, filled in with 740,000 cubic metres of dredged sand. The processing tents at Western Jet Foil are behind covered fences, warning notices and cameras. Now the only ways to photograph anyone involved in the small boats, beyond dim shapes on an unmarked coach, is to use a drone or take long-lens pictures from the Lord Warden. This is why the quality of the images telling the story of the small boats has become poorer: the people rescued from the sea are even further away from us, and they look it. The whole crisis, at least on the English side of the Channel, has all but disappeared behind barricades. The ground itself, the very threshold of Britain, is obscured. Online maps currently show docks and channels which no longer exist. There is nothing to see and no one to question, beyond a couple of personnel manning the gates. With their eyes on each other, and the cameras on them, neither could speak frankly. I let them be. There are no lone security guards waiting to confide Dover's true feelings now.

And so everything here has changed, except what Dover does. Almost out of sight, now, Dover is still rescuing, landing and feeding people recovered from the Channel, just as it has always done since first we came by sea.

Notes

Chapter 1

Mitie: Mitie Group PLC 'Full year results for the year ended 31 March 2024' (6 June 2024)

'A record year of delivery; entering new 'Facilities Transformation' Three-Year Plan with good momentum: Results presentation for the year ended 31 March 2024' Mitie Group powerpoint presentation: Page 32 (6 June 2024)

Chapter 2

Headlines: Charles Hymas, 'Home Office spends £6,000 slice of immigration budget on Domino's pizzas for Channel migrants' *The Daily Telegraph* (8 October 2021)

Chief Inspector of Borders report: 'An inspection of the initial processing of migrants arriving via small boats at Tug Haven and Western Jet Foil December 2021–January 2022' David Neal, Independent Chief Inspector of Borders and Immigration, Presented to Parliament pursuant to Section 50(2) of the UK Borders Act 2007 July 2022

Chapter 3

Clearsprings: Mark Wilding, 'The Asylum King', *Prospect* (9 July 2024)

Chapter 4

UK funding French police: Jamie Grierson, 'UK to pay £55m to French border patrols to fund migrant clampdown', *The Guardian* (20 July 2021)

French police: Elaine Ganley, 'French police suicide rate climbs, French govt is flummoxed', *Associated Press* (18 August 2019)

Refugee health: 'Mental health support for refugees and people seeking asylum', Refugee Council www.refugeecouncil.org.uk/our-work/mental-health-support-for-refugees-and-people-seeking-asylum/ (accessed 9 March 2025)

Chapter 5

Michael Gove: Hansard (HC) Volume 710: debated on Monday 14 March 2022

Attitudes to refugees 2022: Isabell Kirk, 'Are attitudes to Ukrainian refugees unique?' *YouGov* (12 July 2022)

Attitudes to migration 2025: Matthew Smith, 'Where public opinion stands at the beginning of 2025' *YouGov* (2 January 2025)

Migration key to growth: Office for Budget Responsibility Briefing paper No.8 'Forecasting potential output – the supply side of the economy' November 2022

Cost of UK asylum system: National Audit Office 'An Overview of the Home Office for the new Parliament 2023–24' October 2024

Chapter 6

Robert Jenrick: Peter Walker, 'The three housing controversies Robert Jenrick is facing down' *The Guardian* (25 June 2020); Billy Kenber, 'Tories gave Robert Jenrick home renovation the go-ahead,' *The Times* (24 June 2020)

Legal Migration: Office for National Statistics, 'Long-term international migration, provisional: year ending June 2023' (23 November 2023)

Sudanese grant rate: Home Office, 'How many people are granted asylum in the UK?' (28 November 2024)

Manston conditions: Flora Thompson, 'Watchdog describes unsafe and wretched conditions at migrants processing centre' *The Independent* (26 October 2022)

Braverman deal; ayslum backlog: Paul Seddon, 'UK strikes revised deal with France on Channel migrants' BBC News Online (14 November 2022)

Chapter 7

Bibby Stockholm claims: Catriona Stewart, 'Bibby Stockholm asylum barge claims are 'false', says CEO' *The Herald* (20 July 2023)

CTM contract: Lizzie Dearden, 'Government quietly awards travel firm £1.6bn contract for asylum barges and accommodation' *The Independent* (16 June 2023)

Darwin: Nora Barlow [Darwin], Lady Barlow (ed.) 'The Works of Charles Darwin, Vol. 1: Diary of the Voyage of H.M.S. Beagle' (Published online March 2017)

Chapter 8

Eritrean claims granted: Home Office, 'How many people are granted asylum in the UK?' (28 November 2024)

UK genetics: Wellcome Trust: 'Who do you think you really are? The first fine-scale genetic map of the British Isles,' from Leslie S et al. 'The fine-scale genetic structure of the British population.' *Nature* 2015.

Rates of volunteering: Official Statistics: Community Life Survey 2023/24: 'Volunteering and charitable giving' Department for Culture, Media and Sport (4 December 2024)

Chapter 13

Serco contract and profits: Tom Howard, 'Serco wins largest-ever contract from UK government worth £1.9bn' *Proactive Investors* (8 January 2019)

Cost of asylum system: National Audit Office Report, 'Value for money – Investigation into asylum accommodation' (20 March 2024)

Serco and Mears profits: Matt Dathan, 'Migrants will be put up in hotels for years yet, Treasury admits' *The Sunday Times* (23 March 2025)

Clearsprings profits: Diane Taylor, 'Profits of Home Office asylum housing provider rise to £90m a year' *The Guardian* (3 November 2024)

Chapter 14

Charity Commission investigation: Charity Commission for England and Wales – 'Decision: Charity Inquiry: Care4Calais' (24 August 2023)

Boris Johnson on blocked Rwanda flight: EIN, 'Bar Council and Law Society warn that Prime Minister's attacks on immigration lawyers are misleading and dangerous' *Electronic Immigration Network* (14 June 2022)

Braverman quote: Charles Hymas, 'Braverman: Some charities are 'politically motivated activists masquerading as humanitarians' *The Daily Telegraph* (24 August 2023)

Chapter 15

Rwanda cost: Home Office transparency data, 'Breakdown of Home Office costs associated with the MEDP with Rwanda and the Illegal Migration Act 2023' (2 December 2024)

Global Initiative Against Transnational Organised Crime: 'Small boats, big business – the industrialisation of crosschannel migrant smuggling' (February 2024)

Smuggling trial: BBC News online, 'Merchants of death' people-smuggling gang jailed' (5 November 2024)

Numbers crossing: Migration Observatory, 'People crossing the English Channel in small boats' (28 Jun 2024)

Attitudes: IPSOS, Keiran Pedley, '6 in 10 Britons hold unfavourable opinion of Donald Trump and Elon Musk' (18 January 2025)

Attitudes to safe routes: British Future, 'Public gives new government a chance on immigration reforms – with space to go further too' (14 July 2024) www.britishfuture.org/public-gives-new-government-a-chance-on-immigration-reforms/ (accessed 23 March 2025)

National attitudes to immigration, and Reform confusion: Sunder Katwala, Steve Ballinger, Heather Rolfe and Jake Puddle, 'Restoring trust in polarised times: Immigration in the new parliament. Findings from the Ipsos/British Future immigration attitudes tracker' *British Future* (19 September 2024)

Reform voters: Gaby Hinsliff, 'Nigel Farage feels real': why young British men are drawn to Reform' *The Guardian* (8 March 2025)

Tunisia/Libya attacks: Emma Wallis, 'Did the Tunisian coastguard ram a migrant boat and cause 52 people to drown?' *InfoMigrants* (22 November 2024)

French attacks on Channel boats: Nicola Kelly, May Bulman, Tomas Statius, Bashar Deeb and Fahim Abed, 'Revealed: UK-funded French forces putting migrants' lives at risk with small-boat tactics' *The Observer* (23 March 2024)

Allowing asylum seekers to work: Alun Humphrey, Helena Wilson, Robert Ford, 'BSA 41: Immigration Changing attitudes, policy preferences and partisanship' National Centre for Social Research (12 June 2024)

Rejoin Europe: Dylan Difford, 'How do Britons feel about Brexit five years on?' *YouGov* (Jan 29 2025)

Turning from America to Europe: Policy Institute, King's College London 'Europe, not America, now favoured as ally for Britain – in reversal from almost 60 years ago, study finds' (23 January 2025)

Climate migration: Gaia Vince, 'Is the world ready for mass migration due to climate change?' *BBC Future* (18 November 2022)

Acknowledgements

This book is based on work first commissioned by the *Financial Times Weekend* Life & Arts section, versions of which appear here, with kind permission. Huge thanks and admiration to my editors there: Lorien Kite, Horatia Harrod, Alec Russell, Janine Gibson and Tom Robbins. What an honour it is to write for you. There are plenty of reasons why the FT is one of the world's best newspapers: you are five of them. Special thanks to Alec for that first go-ahead and for your wonderful support always; to Janine for the *Bibby Stockholm* commission; and especially to Lorien for your tireless editing and guidance – and for handling my working method so adroitly and with such humour. (The moment when you gently forbade me from boarding the *Bibby Stockholm* without permission and from the sea remains a favourite.) Great thanks and mighty respect to legendary picture editor Hilary Kirby and sublime photographer Harry Mitchell. It is a privilege to work with you.

This is a work of praise and gratitude for the astonishing courage, determination, resilience and indomitable humanity of Clare Moseley, Gessica Lastrucci, Cosi Doerfel-Hill, Kay Marsh and the remarkable people who work and volunteer alongside them, and across the field of refugee support. My sincere thanks to you for your time and trouble. A deep bow to you and a huge cheer, on all our behalves, for being what is still great about Britain.

Without the truly exceptional kindness, faith, support, patience and understanding of Gracie and Adrian Cooper at Little Toller this book would never have been. Thank you both, so much, and thank you Jon Woolcott! What a team you truly are. My thanks to Holly Ovenden for your most gorgeous cover.

Great thanks, always, for peerless guidance, trouble and time to Phoebe Wyatt and my most brilliant agent, Zoe Waldie, at Rogers, Colderidge and White.

For sustaining the author through the usual storms, and for your light always, all thanks to my dear friends and extended family: Doug Field, Ellie Hunt, Rob Ketteridge, Roger Couhig, Mo Bakaya, Alison Finch, Anna Gavalda, Emma Close, Femi Oyebode, Rebecca Shooter, Matt Gallop, Jeremy Grange, Julian May, Dan Richards, Jeff Young, Amy Buscombe, Rob Macfarlane, Chris Kenyon, Richard Hirst, Luke Arch, Galiia Bektemirova, John McAuliffe, Jeanette Winterson, Niall Griffiths, Sophy Roberts, Anna Rose Hughes, Merlin Hughes, David and Kim Maylor, and Alexander Clare and Sally Clare; thank you especially dear Ma!

And with all my love, and deep gratitude and admiration for the fighting resolve you both demonstrate and inspire, thank you, dearest Aubrey and darling Esther. You make me feel so very lucky. With all my heart, thank you. This is for you x

H. C.
Hebden Bridge, 2025

Oliver Rackham Library
THE ASH TREE
ANCIENT WOODS OF THE HELFORD RIVER
ANCIENT WOODS OF SOUTH-EAST WALES

Richard Mabey Library
NATURE CURE
THE UNOFFICIAL COUNTRYSIDE
BEECHCOMBINGS
GILBERT WHITE: A BIOGRAPHY

Nature Classics
THROUGH THE WOODS *H. E. Bates*
WANDERERS IN THE NEW FOREST *Juliette de Baïracli Levy*
MEN AND THE FIELDS *Adrian Bell*
THE ALLOTMENT *David Crouch & Colin Ward*
ISLAND YEARS, ISLAND FARM *Frank Fraser Darling*
AN ENGLISH FARMHOUSE *Geoffrey Grigson*
THE MAKING OF THE ENGLISH LANDSCAPE *W. G. Hoskins*
A SHEPHERD'S LIFE *W. H. Hudson*
WILD LIFE IN A SOUTHERN COUNTY *Richard Jefferies*
FOUR HEDGES *Clare Leighton*
DREAM ISLAND *R. M. Lockley*
RING OF BRIGHT WATER *Gavin Maxwell*
COPSFORD *Walter Murray*
THE FAT OF THE LAND *John Seymour*
IN PURSUIT OF SPRING *Edward Thomas*
THE NATURAL HISTORY OF SELBORNE *Gilbert White*

Field Notes & Monographs
AUROCHS AND AUKS *John Burnside*
ORISON FOR A CURLEW *Horatio Clare*
SOMETHING OF HIS ART: WALKING WITH J. S. BACH *Horatio Clare*
BROTHER.DO.YOU.LOVE.ME *Manni and Reuben Coe*
HERBACEOUS *Paul Evans*
THE SCREAMING SKY *Charles Foster*
THE TREE *John Fowles*
TIME AND PLACE *Alexandra Harris*
DIARY OF A YOUNG NATURALIST *Dara McAnulty*
THE LONG FIELD *Pamela Petro*
SHALIMAR *Davina Quinlivan*
ELOWEN *William Henry Searle*
SNOW *Marcus Sedgwick*
WATER AND SKY, RIDGE AND FURROW *Neil Sentance*
BLACK APPLES OF GOWER *Iain Sinclair*
ON SILBURY HILL *Adam Thorpe*
GHOST TOWN: A LIVERPOOL SHADOWPLAY *Jeff Young*

Anthology & Biography
ARBOREAL *Adrian Cooper*
MY HOUSE OF SKY: THE LIFE OF J. A. BAKER *Hetty Saunders*
NO MATTER HOW MANY SKIES HAVE FALLEN *Ken Worpole*
GOING TO GROUND *Jon Woolcott*

Little Toller Books
w. littletoller.co.uk E. books@littletoller.co.uk